"Using familiar examples from daily life, this clearly written book examines the intricacies of economic and ecological cycles. Cloutier not only effectively demonstrates the relevance of these issues to daily suburban life, but shows how choices that affirm human dignity over individualism, and the bonds of community over empty excess, are both practical and spiritually renewing. *Walking God's Earth* is a faithful call for Catholics to take the steps they can, attentively and patiently working to renew the structures of our lives together for the refreshment of all creation. His vision of green and walkable communities inspires hope that Americans can renew our ways of living together, walking through God's creation as our own shared, and livable, home."

—Erin Lothes Biviano
Assistant Professor of Theology
College of Saint Elizabeth
Morristown, NJ

Walking God's Earth

The Environment and Catholic Faith

David Cloutier

LITURGICAL PRESS
Collegeville, Minnesota

www.litpress.org

1   2   3   4   5   6   7   8   9

Library of Congress Cataloging-in-Publication Data

Cloutier, David M., 1972–
    Walking God's earth : the environment and Catholic faith / David Cloutier.
        pages   cm
    Includes bibliographical references.
    ISBN 978-0-8146-3709-8 — ISBN 978-0-8146-3734-0 (ebook)
    1. Human ecology—Religious aspects—Catholic Church. 2. Catholic Church—Doctrines. I. Title.

BX1795.H82C56 2014
261.8'8—dc23   2014014777

Contents

Acknowledgments   vii

Introduction: Finding Our Place   ix

Part One

    1. Beauty   3

    2. Losing Our Place   12

    3. Basic Theology I: Creation and Covenant   27

    4. Basic Theology II: Redemption and Renewal   41

Transition: What, Then, Shall We Do?   53

Part Two

    5. Food and Fuel   63

    6. The Country and the City   85

    7. Work and Play   94

    8. The Global Economy   104

Conclusion: Making Places Holy   117

Notes   127

Bibliography   139

Acknowledgments

It is tempting to thank everyone who has played a role in my development from an urban child with little sense of the natural world to a Catholic advocate for living in harmony with the created world. Without them, there would be no book. But their presence is indicated in the text. Here, I would just like to extend thanks to those who helped this book come together. Barry Hudock at Liturgical Press proposed this idea to me at a fortuitous time, during a sabbatical, and I leapt at the chance to put together something that would make this theology more available to the church. He, Andy Edwards, and Stephanie Lancour at the Press have all done great work on this book. I also want to thank my institution, Mount St. Mary's University, and a generous grant from the Louisville Institute, for the sabbatical that left just enough space for me to entertain a second book project. I wrote and edited much of the text at the library of Hood College—the friendly help of the librarians in sharing their resources enabled me to minimize my commute, down to a walk across the street! My dear colleagues and friends Julie Hanlon Rubio and Diane Millis made helpful suggestions on parts of the text. Finally, I am so indebted to my experience of four years at Carleton College. Carleton has great students, great faculty, stimulating classrooms, and an ongoing institutional commitment to the environment. But much more important, it simply sets up different patterns of life. *Living* those patterns allows a glimpse at what could be. That kind of hope is so necessary in addressing the challenges we face.

Introduction

Finding Our Place

The duty to emphasize an appropriate catechesis concerning creation, in order to recall the meaning and religious significance of protecting it . . . can have an important impact on the perception of the value of life itself as well as on the satisfactory solution of the consequent inevitable social problems.

—Benedict XVI[1]

First, go out and take a walk. Really, just walk. No smartphone, no car, no destination. Just you and your own two feet. Go.

Walking is perhaps our most fundamental way of being in the world. Abraham was a wandering Aramaean. Moses walked with the Israelites for forty years through the desert. Jesus had "nowhere to rest his head" (Luke 9:58) and took a final walk to his death on a cross. Scientists tell us that a major evolutionary reason why humans have such large brains is that they walk on two legs and free up their hands for toolmaking, for a new way of interacting with the world. And modern self-improvement gurus will point out that one of our worst cultural habits is how much we sit.

When you walk, wherever you are walking, I'd call your attention to two things—things you will notice because you are going slowly, connected to the ground, grounded. First, notice all the *variety* around you. Varieties of colors, countless differing trees and flowers and grasses, different creatures scurrying or flying around. Green, white, blue, pink, brown, black—or maybe you see the indescribable array of autumn colors. Notice the pitch of the ground—sloping up or down, perhaps toward a creek or a hill. Look up at the sky—the clouds differ in shape and texture; perhaps there is darkness gathering in one direction, contrasting with the clear blue elsewhere. Or perhaps it is night, with the waxing and waning moon and the endless constellations of stars that fascinated the ancients. And don't just look: listen for all the sounds of the creatures and the wind, smell the unexpected scents, touch all the myriad textures. Maybe there's even something to taste.

Amidst all this amazing variety, around us all the time and accessible within a few blocks, notice something else: notice how *small* you are. Sure, the ants crawling underfoot are smaller (though their swarming sometimes seems unstoppable). But compare yourself to the sky or the trees. Try to imagine buildings as tall as the mountains on the horizon. Try to think how far it is just to the moon, much less the sun, ninety-three million miles away. Try to imagine the tremendous force of the blowing wind, the shining sun, the ever-flowing water. And—this works best in the woods, but it applies to your neighborhood too—try to think about how all this goes on and on and on, mostly all by itself.

Now, hopefully your walk was something like mine—early May, a leafy Maryland town on a creek with mountains on the horizon, after a morning rain, sunny but with those clouds creeping in again. But maybe you listened, and all you heard was some guy's leaf blower. Maybe it's January, and the sense of variety is . . . less obvious. Or maybe you walked out of a bookstore into a huge mall parking lot or into Times Square. Leaf blowers, asphalt, even January—there's something to learn here, too, although perhaps the insights are about *absences*.

The real lessons are about the sheer abundance and vastness of what is right outside your door, even in our developed age. This is a sheer abundance that *we did not make*—we may have *tended* it, but we did not make it—and it is gifted to us in the most direct, immediate, and constant way, that is, if we are walking and paying attention. Learning how to walk with this vision of vast abundance is at the heart of what this book explores: a Catholic understanding of the environment.

This first lesson, I think, is really hard to learn in the abstract, simply from pretty words on a page. We learn it by seeing it embodied in specific, *particular* places. I learned it by taking a specific walk, which inspired me to realize what to write in starting this book. This emphasis on particularity matters theologically too. The whole biblical story points us to the experience of particulars—the particular people and land, the particular Person of Christ. Even today, Catholicism recognizes that there is no people called "the church" other than in the particular *place* people gather around a bishop for the Eucharist. We meet Christ specifically, not in the abstract; we meet him as Lord and Friend, not as philosopher or idea. So too we learn God's creation in the particular.

What do I mean by this focus on the particular, and how it is necessary for the proper study of Catholic teaching on the environment? Let me offer two examples from my own life history, which suggest awareness of the particularities of creation, as well as the variety of forms such awareness might take. The first is growing up in Chicago, in the city. Chicago's motto is *Urbs in horto*, City in a Garden. Since much of Chicago was built during an era of urban planning called the "City Beautiful" movement, it has certain features that characterized that movement—parks, trees, and the like. True, it's a city, and it has many environmental embarrassments typical of cities. But two natural features captivated me while growing up. One was the extraordinary, hundred-year-old oak tree right outside my house, between the sidewalk and the street. As a child, the tree seemed indescribably gigantic. The trunk was huge—you could easily hide behind it—and its branches stretched up and out beyond any other tree on the block. It was "our tree." The other natural feature, common to all Chicagoans, was "the Lake." In Chicago, physical geography is all about the Lake, the vast expanse where suddenly all the man-made buildings and roads end, and the water just stretches out endlessly. The city goes no farther. It gives Chicago an odd geography: it does not actually expand in all directions, since the city center is right on the Lake. It is limited. Delightfully, the early city planners intentionally decided to keep nearly all of the city's lengthy lakefront free of private development and open to the public. To walk along the Lake through a network of parks, then, was our shared experience of a nature much bigger than even our big city.

However, my real education in nature happened in a second, different place, a small Minnesota college town with a river running through it. The campus itself lacked the splendid, pristine quads of other colleges—the central area was called "the Bald Spot," because it was flooded for broomball on ice every winter! But what it had was a walkable town with a remarkably intact old-fashioned Main Street on one side, and an eight-hundred-acre arboretum on the other, with trails off into the woods that eventually petered out into farm fields. Oh, and a campus rule that virtually disallowed cars. Hence, we all lived a walking life, with town on one side and wilderness on the other. That world was not actually very big, but it seemed enormous on foot. You could *drive* from the far end of the Main Street to the farthest reaches of the Arb in five to ten minutes. But on *foot*, it was rich, varied, and seemingly endless. And truly beautiful.

There's something else to notice about these places: I *lived* in them, as did others. They weren't strictly speaking "wild," even if the Lake would have drowned a person and the Arb was pitch-dark at night. Having lived in such modest Midwestern places, my first trip to the Pacific Northwest was jaw-dropping in its vast scale (as well as in the forest-destroying clear-cuts I saw for the first time). But I think that it's very important to appreciate the natural wonders of home places, not just of remote tourist sites. It is good to have national parks, but not if we destroy our own home places. Importantly, my home places shared a walking scale, so that the wonders could reveal themselves to us. Farmer and essayist Wendell Berry notes, in an essay titled "Out of Your Car, Off Your Horse," that "properly speaking, global thinking is not possible," because "no one can make ecological good sense globally." All places are naturally different and to some degree unique. Rather, "everyone can make ecological good sense locally, if the affection, the scale, the knowledge, the tools, and the skills are right."[2] Berry is not recommending an NIMBY policy—just keep the landfill, but "Not In My BackYard," shipping the garbage to some poor rural community elsewhere. He is calling us to remember the ability of all of us to care rightly for our local places and tend their beauty, because this is what actually produces "affection."

I begin with a walk and these stories because the idea of a nature we *inhabit and tend*, well or badly, is really the vision best suited to a Catholic theology and spirituality of the environment. It's about a recognition of and wonder at our own particular places, and a renewed recognition of how, too often, we ignore or even degrade their value in our everyday life. Our "walk through" the Catholic tradition will proceed in two parts. The first part of the book introduces the broad spirituality and doctrines on which the tradition is based. We begin by examining more closely our experience of beauty and how this moves our spirit; but we also recognize how our spirits are often distracted and neglectful of this beauty. This loss of our sense of place in a beautiful, ordered creation is due to three spiritual problems: scale, speed, and selfishness. These spiritual counterforces will also be examined. Then we will turn to the basic theological beliefs of Catholics about God, creation, and salvation, drawing especially on the scriptural writings. Various ideas in Christian Scripture can seem to lead to environmental neglect and even destruction. But read properly, the Scriptures reinforce a spirituality of wonder, care, and gift in relation to nature and its abundance.

The second part of the book moves into our lived response. In the transition section, we will see that the Christian life is not simply one of appreciating beauty, but acting on it. We will explore in depth our moral call to live out proper patterns of this vocation as caretakers. Pope Benedict XVI, the "Green Pope," writes, "*Nature expresses a design of love and truth. It is prior to us, and it has been given to us by God as the setting for our life. Nature speaks to us of the Creator* (cf. Rom 1:20) *and his love for humanity. It is destined to be 'recapitulated' in Christ at the end of time* (cf. Eph 1:9-10; Col 1:19-20). *Thus it too is a 'vocation'*" (*Caritas in Veritate* 48). Caring for creation is not a special interest for a few but an integral part of the Christian life for all, because it is based on fundamental beliefs of the faith. Recent papal writings have affirmed that this commitment is essential, not a novel addition or optional extra. From Genesis, which depicts a wholly good creation, in every element, through the incarnation of Jesus in flesh and blood, even to the vision of "the new heavens and new earth" offered in Revelation, the Bible resolutely rejects a purely "spiritual" faith.

However, "being green" and helping the environment can often seem overwhelming. The problems seem so big, the recommended actions so small (and numerous). I propose that we examine four basic patterns that animate our shared life today: how we eat and get energy, how we design our dwelling together, how we balance work and recreation, and how we direct our economic resources. These patterns, as we often practice them in society, are distorted; for the first time in human history, vast numbers of humans live far from any natural rhythm or cycle and have acquired sufficient power to manipulate and even destroy the created order on a large scale. We have stopped working with what Benedict calls "the grammar of creation," and have begun to believe (falsely) that there is no greater grammar within which we live. Our fundamental calling, then, is to identify these distortions and figure out how to resist them and build up alternative patterns. Our journey concludes with a reflection on how such alternative ways of living are ways of real holiness, exemplifying the "universal call to holiness" at the heart of Vatican II's vision of the church.

That is the map for our journey. But here are a couple pre-hike traveling tips so that you avoid some common wrong turns and missteps along the way. The first and most important thing to remember is this: avoid thinking of the environment in either-or, all-or-nothing terms. For example, either we eat, or we preserve nature. Either we drive our cars, or we go back to living in caves. Remember the walk: the world does not exist as this kind of either-or. Dan Misleh, who directs the US bishops' campaign on climate change, begins his talks with an exercise where he asks people to close their eyes and say what images come to mind when he speaks a word: "environment." I saw this happen in the classroom; people respond with all sorts of images, but one image is always absent: people! In our rightful concern about environmental degradation, we can sometimes imagine "humans" and "the environment" as two different things, even as enemies. (A popular environmental book is called *The World Without Us*!)

By contrast, it's essential for a Catholic view to see that we are *participants* in the environment, neither an "invasive species" nor mere disembodied souls. Thus, as we will see, many environmental issues have to do with getting our *scale* right. My opening exercise of walking was an invitation to enter into that proper scale and perhaps a reminder that we are far too removed from that way of experiencing the world. Things tend to go wrong when we lose that sense of scale. We cannot live well on the highest mountain peaks or in vast deserts or under the ocean—nature overwhelms us. But we can overwhelm nature when in our building, our speed, our hunger for harvest, we deplete soils, fisheries, mines, and even the air. We throw off the balance, even as nature still knows how to throw us off balance.

The ultimate choice we must consider as Catholics is whether we are shared *participants* in God's creation or triumphant *tyrants* over it. This is the real choice we face. The man whom many cite as the founder of modern experimental science, Francis Bacon, believed nature and humanity were in a battle. We must use science to achieve genuine power over nature, instead of having it have power over us. We learned nature's secrets through experimentation, but the goal was not to wonder at its marvels. Rather, he wrote, "the true and lawful goal of the sciences is none other than this: that human life be endowed with new discoveries and powers."[3] Wendell Berry describes this presumption to knowledge as a kind of ignorance, where "wonder has been replaced by a research agenda," but an agenda that *ignores* anything like imagination, sympathy, and affection.[4] It reduces nature, so that it can be fully comprehended and controlled by humans. In so doing, it distorts nature. As Pope Benedict writes, nature is "prior to us"; therefore, "reducing nature merely to a collection of contingent data ends up doing violence to the environment" (*Caritas in Veritate* 48).

Of course, Catholics do not follow Francis Bacon but have a different Francis as the patron saint of the environment, St. Francis of Assisi. Our present pope, his papal namesake, explained the name in one of his first audiences: "For me, [Francis] is the man of poverty, the man of peace, the man who loves and protects creation; these days we do not have a very good relationship with creation, do we?"[5] In his homily at the papal inaugural, Pope Francis noted that we all, Christians and non-Christians, must be protectors,

> protecting all creation, the beauty of the created world, as the Book of Genesis tells us and as St. Francis of Assisi showed us. It means respecting each of God's creatures and respecting the environment in which we live. . . . Please, I would like to ask all those who have positions of responsibility in economic, political and social life, and all men and women of goodwill: let us be 'protectors' of creation, protectors of God's plan inscribed in nature, protectors of one another and of the environment. Let us not allow omens of destruction and death to accompany the advance of this world![6]

The vocation explained by terms like "protector" and "steward" displays a fundamentally different stance within the world: not of mastery, but of service. It is a stance that sees in the natural environment not merely "raw material" but God's wisdom, which can teach us if we make careful use of it in sustaining human life.

Another point to keep in mind: concern for the environment should not be seen as something separate from, or in contrast to, other spiritual and moral concerns that are more commonly seen as "Catholic." The environment is not simply an issue, along with a laundry list of others. They are all connected. In fact, many of the Catholic teachings on life and sexuality are rooted in the same soil as Catholic environmental teaching: respecting and protecting nature, rather than doing whatever we want with it. When we see the larger natural world as something we can exploit however we want, we end up doing the same to human bodies, "encouraging activity that fails to respect human nature itself" (*Caritas in Veritate* 48). Recent popes have described this as *an essential connection between "human ecology" and "natural ecology."* The desire to master the world, to dominate it, to impose our will, to make our own choice, to manipulate God's ordering—these are the same sinful diseases that drive Catholicism to cry out against abortion, euthanasia, the death penalty, cloning, sexual promiscuity, and the victimization of the poor and vulnerable. The Catholic tradition believes, as Benedict puts it, that "the book of nature is one and indivisible: it takes in not only the environment but also life, sexuality, marriage, the family, social relations: in a word, integral human development. Our duties towards the environment are linked to our duties towards the human person. . . . It would be wrong to uphold one set of duties while trampling on the other" (ibid., 51). As we will see, other basic commandments against lying, stealing, and coveting are routinely broken in the course of our excessive abuse of nature. If we genuinely shared property, used it moderately, and depicted truthfully the impact of our lives on nature, we would certainly do less harm! Thus, both spiritually and morally, our environmental lives are intimately linked to the basic morality of our faith. Part of the task of this book is to help us see these connections more clearly, in hopes that God's desire for "the renewal of the earth" may be more and more realized in our own desires and in the practices of our communities.

So, off we go!

Part One

chapter 1

Beauty

We need to be re-educated in wonder and in the ability to recognize the beauty made manifest in created realities.

—Benedict XVI[1]

The created world is beautiful. This beauty can be so arresting and powerful that our human ancestors marked out certain natural places and forces as spiritual or holy—the sacred tree or stone, the mountaintop, even the sun and the moon. As Mircea Eliade puts it, for a religious person, "space is not homogeneous": it is not all monotonously the same but is rather a map of the sacred, with spiritual power assigned to certain places and objects.[2] We should not imagine our ancestors actually believed that trees were gods. What they sensed was that nature made the spiritual appear, connecting us to its larger force and power. True, this idea could lead further, toward superstitious thinking—toward the idea that by manipulating the object, one could manipulate the divine power itself for one's own advantage. But today's religions can be used in this false way too—as a manipulation of the divine, rather than a recognition of a transcendent power that is beyond us. Authentic religious experience is not of *control*, but of *reception* and connection, of tapping into something larger and wiser. Such receptivity to God can be found through receptivity to nature's bewitching and beguiling beauty.

Christianity has at times forgotten this basic insight into the spiritual power of nature's beauty and focused instead on doctrines, or even on purely invisible souls. It's important for us to remember that the first story of Scripture is an extraordinary story about the sheer goodness of the created order made by God. Doctrines and souls are important, of course. But it is not with these that our human religious journey begins. It is with the experience of beauty. Hans Urs von Balthasar, one of the greatest twentieth-century Catholic theologians, begins his fifteen-volume theology not with dogmas or morals, but with "theological aesthetics"—the importance of the experience of grasping and being grasped by beauty.[3] Balthasar is recovering an ancient impulse, also seen in the philosophical statement that "all philosophy begins in wonder." Scientists also experience this. Scripture scholar William Brown sees this "overwhelming sense of wonder" that scientists confess as "what unites the empiricist and the contemplator, the scientist and the believer."[4] Balthasar's work, writes Anthony Ciorra, insists that a modern world that has lost a sense of God "would find God by listening to what God has created."[5]

But what does it mean to say something is "beautiful"? Let us consider three dimensions of our experience of beauty: beauty has a form, beauty reaches out and compels our admiration, and beauty draws us in to learn more about its intricacy.

The first point is recognizing that beauty has a form. Balthasar's first volume is subtitled *Seeing the Form*. The Latin word for beauty is *formosa*. "Form" is a difficult word—we deride "form letters" and worry when someone acts too "formal." Why is "form" so crucial for beauty? We can grasp its meaning first by thinking about how the world looks in a fog, or when our vision becomes blurred, or even when light is dim and indirect. We cannot really "see," because seeing means recognizing and distinguishing certain shapes and their relationships.

The idea of form is especially captured in human terms by considering what it means to see the uniqueness of a face. Human faces are remarkably distinctive, and their forms mark us more than anything else in terms of our identity. The Old Testament is filled with passages expressing longing to "see the face of God" or pleas to God to "let your countenance shine forth." Why God's face? This is a way of expressing what it means to see someone's true form, for their true identity and beauty to be revealed. To see "face-to-face" is really the culmination of what it means to see. John O'Donohue reminds us that "the first thing the new infant sees is the human face" and nothing else we see will ever "rival the significance of the face."[6] The face here represents the form of the person. It is telling that our driver's licenses and course rosters have head shots for identification purposes! It is telling that when we meet someone, we look into his or her face; compare this to two dogs meeting at the park! One of the greatest nature psalms highlights the relation of God's face to the whole of creation:

> When you hide your face, they panic.
> > Take away their breath, they perish
> > and return to the dust.
> Send forth your spirit, they are created
> > and you renew the face of the earth. (Ps 104:29-30)

The face has a pattern, a form, and O'Donohue notes that it is this "hidden order and rhythm of pattern" that is the foundation of beauty.[7] Such delightful form can also be found elsewhere: consider the form of games, works of art, music, and dance. To perceive beauty in the activity, we must see the form. This is why (unfortunately) many people consider baseball "boring"! Our world delights us insofar as we see the form.

So let's ask ourselves, are we looking at the whole of creation in this way? The created world has an intricate, complex form—Pope Benedict calls it a "grammar," which "sets forth criteria for its wise use, not its reckless exploitation" (*Caritas in Veritate* 48).[8] Learning nature is like learning the complexities of a spoken language . . . or of baseball! Saint Basil praises God for the gift of human intelligence, for its ability "to learn of the great wisdom of the artificer from the most insignificant objects of creation . . . the tiniest of plants and animals."[9] Much of human history has involved humans discovering how to become fluent in this language. Take the ancient art of beekeeping. Attention to the bees reveals the extraordinary intricacy of their lives. Bill McKibben explains that, among many other practices, beehives deal with summer heat with "a primitive form of air conditioning": when it gets too hot, some bees bring back water drops, and then they all stop their work and beat their wings together to evaporate the water.[10] Or consider the "beehive democracy" when a hive gets too full and bees must go out and find a new hive—a complex process of decision making involving numerous "scouts" who then return and start "dances" that correspond to how good various possible sites might be.[11] Over time, more and more bees gravitate to the better dances, and a decision is made together. McKibben connects all this to the real-life story of small Vermont beekeeper Kirk Webster, who carefully observes the ins and outs of his hives, working with their natural processes, helping them along, and reaping some sweet rewards in the process. And of course, the wider world reaps the rewards, too, since bees pollinate hundreds of fruits and flowers. While Mr. Webster helps the bees, he doesn't make their lives. The form is not something we as humans made up; rather, it is given to us, as one of millions of processes that make up "nature."

Now, bees may make you run away, so we must look to other examples for our second point: that beauty overwhelms us in reaching out and almost *demanding* our admiration. Consider the experience of California redwoods or the Rocky Mountains: in our society, we are still captivated by natural beauty and sometimes overwhelmed by its power, even its sacredness. Beauty like this has a kind of force, power, or inherent attractiveness—a luminosity or splendor—that moves us. We could say it overpowers us. It awes us. It has a kind of magnetism. It is like the (very few!) days when the weather is "perfect." As Balthasar writes of beauty, it "brings with it a self-evidence that en-lightens without mediation"—that is, its "form is so constituted as to be able to mediate from within itself the light that illuminates its beauty."[12]

These breathtaking moments are reminders of the ancient Catholic idea of the analogy of being. This very abstract-sounding term simply means that we experience ourselves and things in the world as a part of some vastly larger whole, something prior to ourselves and deserving of recognition, and even reverence. We can't fully understand it, but we just *know* something special is there. Existence itself is a great mystery—not in the sense of something unknown, but something with infinite depth, like looking down into the sea. As Balthasar puts it, God has made all things "with the grace of participation in the inexhaustibility of its origin. It bears within itself a wealth that cannot be consumed like a finite sum of money. You are never finished with any being, be it the tiniest gnat or the most inconspicuous stone. It has a secret opening, through which flow never-failing replenishments of sense and significance ceaselessly flowing to it from eternity."[13] It is always possible to harden our hearts against beauty, but it involves effort. (By the way, this is why so much environmental harm must be hidden from sight, often elaborately.)

This feeling of being grasped by beauty should lead to certain spiritual responses: humility, gratitude, and thanksgiving. For this is all a gift. We didn't make the beautiful day, the sun, the soil that regenerates the grasses. Beauty is like a gift in its sheer excessiveness. It is so much more than we might expect, and we respond best by appreciating it. Beauty is grace, and grace asks only to be received. It is way bigger than what we could have made.

For Christians, God's grace is made manifest in many ways. But we should not forget that a primary experience of it is in creation. Jame Schaefer quotes St. Augustine's praise in *The City of God* for "the manifold diversity of beauty in sky and earth and sea; the abundance of light, and its miraculous loveliness, in sun and moon and stars; the dark shades of woods, the color and fragrance of flowers; the multitudinous varieties of birds, with their songs and their bright plumage; the countless living creatures of all shapes and sizes."[14] Augustine is merely echoing the psalmist, who sings the various beauties of creation, and concludes:

> How varied are your works, LORD!
>> In wisdom you have made them all;
>> the earth is full of your creatures. (Ps 104:24)

These momentary experiences of overwhelming beauty are important, but they are not the whole story. Think about our national parks, for example. The parks themselves—most often remote, forbidding, rocky, dreadfully hot or cold—capture both the power of nature's beauty and our sometimes limited ability to see it. In these places, we feel some of the rawest power of nature, almost like an emotional "pow" moment. Like our romantic movies, though, we gaze fascinated by the "pow" moment of emotional impact and then forget to develop the far more complicated knowledge involved in *lifelong love* of others. C. S. Lewis notes the many great seekers of romantic love are not interested in loving a person; what they love is the immediate experience, the thrill, of falling in love.[15] Correspondingly, we can fall into the trap of thinking natural beauty is *only* experienced in remote places, where we get the "pow." We then neglect nature's beautiful form that is all around us. Much of nature (also like love) involves the humble, difficult task of daily care. Our word "humility" comes from the word for "soil." The form of nature's beauty might not be best captured by gazing up at majestic mountaintops, but in the soil beneath our feet.

Is dirt beautiful? What about those nasty bees? Yes, everything is, but we probably need to *learn* to see its beauty. Thus, our third point: while nature's beauty can pack a kind of irresistible punch, it *also* requires an active response to this invitation—learning better and better to appreciate its amazing form in everything around us. If it is only mountains and eagles that move us, we can be certain that we will go on neglecting and destroying the equally beautiful and intricate bees and prairies, not to mention our own (mostly urban) spaces. Take the bee example: when I see a bee, it is not a "pow" moment—I think of avoiding getting stung! I need to learn from others that there is a form that requires respect and appreciation. Schaefer, in surveying patristic and medieval texts on the beauty of creation, calls this theme "cognitive appreciation brought about when contemplating the harmonious functioning of creatures."[16] She notes how the medieval theologian Hugh of St. Victor reflects on seeing God's handiwork in nature: Some look at the world like "unlettered people" who "see an open book" and can "see the characters, but do not know the letters." When looking at the beauty of nature, they only see the "external appearance" but fail to grasp the "inner meaning" that reflects "the wisdom of the Creator."[17] Today, we must learn again to be literate in the language of God's earth, in order to grasp its beauty.

In order to enter into nature's beauty, let us not simply take pilgrimages to national parks, the "cathedrals" of the natural world. Let us also see the form in our home "parishes" and local regions. There's still a "pow" here, but it's a little more intellectual, more like what we experience when we learn the intricacies of a musical score or football play strategies. A great example of this "cognitive appreciation" of beauty is given by physicist Chet Raymo, who teaches the history of the natural world through what he has observed on his daily walk to work through a one-mile estate-turned-nature-preserve in New England. Raymo notes that after thirty-seven years, knowledge of this landscape "is in my bones" and yet every day still turns up "something noteworthy," because "every pebble and wildflower has a story to tell."[18] He is able to take details of this journey and connect them to large-scale geological and evolutionary history, to distant stars, and even to the varieties of human making that have inhabited the place. As he writes, "A minute lived attentively can contain a millennium; an adequate step can span the planet," and a mile-long walk can traverse territory "as big as the universe."[19] Let us find those close-to-home places where we can savor such walks.

Another especially important but forgotten learning that we need to recover is the form of farming with nature. Food writer Michael Pollan, in *The Omnivore's Dilemma*, made Virginia farmer Joel Salatin a classic example of this skill. Salatin's medium-sized Virginia farm started as a degraded and worn-out set of hills and valleys. On 100 acres, Salatin now produces "40,000 pounds of beef, 30,000 pounds of pork, 10,000 broilers, 1,200 turkeys, 1,000 rabbits, and 35,000 dozen eggs."[20] The meat alone would give 2,000 people 75 pounds each annually, and over 17 dozen eggs. His inputs? Salatin says, "I'm a grass farmer"—that is, virtually the whole farm output, outside of a small amount of chicken feed, comes from a single input: grass. Well, grass . . . and an intricate choreography of moveable pens and coops that enables Salatin to graze each portion of the field just the right amount (and with the right amount of, ahem, "leavings") so that it can then regenerate and again be grazed. As Salatin puts it, "We should call ourselves sun farmers. The grass is just the way we capture solar energy."[21] But the process is by no means automatic. Indeed, it relies on not violating "the law of the second bite" that happens when cows graze one field continuously, using up the grasses they like and allowing species they don't like to take over. To follow this law requires intense human "seeing"—to each section of pasture, to the difference in "recovery times" depending on season and weather, and to the cows themselves, who must be constantly transferred (then the chickens are ported in to eat the bugs out of the cow leavings, and leave their own). Pollan calls the entire operation a matter of "practicing complexity," and Salatin notes that "everything's connected to everything else, so you can't change one thing without changing ten other things."[22] The outcome is simple: a lot of very good food for almost nothing. This kind of farm is certainly capable of matching the output per acre of large operations, perhaps even surpassing it, in terms of variety.[23] But the beautiful outcome requires intense attention to how nature can be coaxed to produce such pure gifts.

One might wish we trained all our farmers with the skill that we expect from doctors and physicists; maybe if we paid them well enough, we would! Sadly, however, nearly nothing in our ordinary food system actually looks like this. In our society, much farming, especially of livestock and poultry, is as machine-like as possible from start to finish—from huge, constantly lit sheds to chickens that cannot stand because they are designed to bulk up as quickly as possible to concrete-walled slaughter-houses with processes that horrify the ordinary person (if they saw them). This is not nature's beauty, but the opposite.

Why is this so? We will need to explore why, but a big part is because, to follow Salatin's process, there is an ineradicable human element, since the beauty of the process must be observed with the kind of intensity and care that the poet uses to choose words or the composer uses for notes. It is an intellectual process, but not a "logical" one. It is not a mechanical one. Working with nature's beauty is a kind of craft process, which can be made more efficient but relies on human attention, skill, and pacing. It is more like teaching or medicine at its best and thus has a labor intensity that we have sought to escape. If nature is as beautiful and bountiful as described here, why have we sought to escape working with it and in it? Why are most of us unlikely to want a job where we tend nature's beauty? In short, why have we lost our sense of this form and our place in it?

chapter 2

Losing Our Place

*At present, in the face of great threats to the
natural environment, we want to express
our concern at the negative consequences for
humanity and for the whole of creation which can
result from economic and technological progress
that does not know its limits.*

—Benedict XVI[1]

I once attended a local talk here in Maryland by a small farmer,
sponsored by the Sierra Club. She presented a fantastic slide
show of all the great things she was doing on her farm. The
place was in fact beautiful; in particular, she had preserved a
mix of woodlots and fields that was not only picture-postcard
charming but also produced all sorts of environmental benefits.
One slide showed a picture of a deer emerging from a woodland.
The farmer then spoke of the problems with the exploding deer
population eating her crops, and someone in the audience piped
up, "What do you do about that?" She paused, and said, "Well,
you're not gonna like it." The laughter in the roomful of Sierra
Club types was a telling mixture of mirth and nervousness!

Nature's dynamic beauty is not the only experience we have.
Deer destroy crops. Bees sting. This is where rhapsodies about
unspoiled nature go wrong. Nature may have beauty, but even
if we learn to see it well, nature can also be a rough place. It

doesn't always seem to be a place of peace and harmony. Even the beekeeper has to wear protective clothing! Those places of knockout natural beauty, "pure nature," are very inhospitable to human beings. Some of the most beautiful natural places—the purple mountain majesties, the wide-open prairie, the oceans—are also very hostile. It's no accident that we don't live in Death Valley (the name!) or on Mount Everest; after a soggy, chilly night camping close to home, it's even clear why we don't all set up tents and sleep under the stars in the woods! If nature is such a gift from God, why does its form often seem like such a threat? If nature is so beautiful, why does so much of civilization seem like a justified "fight" to "tame nature"?

Here we need to make a distinction. On the one hand, theologians sometimes speak about so-called "natural evil"—earthquakes, hurricanes, mass extinctions throughout geological time, the supposed bloodiness of "survival of the fittest," of Tennyson's poetic description of nature as "red in tooth and claw," evoking the predatory cycle of lion and lamb. There is much debate about these "natural evils." Is it a great mystery, all in fact "good" despite our incomprehension, as God seems to tell Job? Is it simply a misrepresentation, as some have argued about the actual importance of species cooperation, not all-out competition, in evolution? Or is it all the result of the human fall into sin, as seems indicated by the Genesis tale of the snake's cursed hostility and Isaiah's future prophecy of the age of the Messiah—lion and lamb lying down together, the child playing by the adder's lair? These issues are complicated, and we will examine them a bit more when we explore the Catholic theology of creation and the Fall in the next chapter.

Here, however, we need to recognize that nature's beauty can be disrupted by *human* evil—by humans failing to see their place (which is not, evidently, in deserts or on mountaintops, except for short times!). When we fail to see our place, we make choices that disrupt the relationships. Even the effects of natural disasters are often related to human failures. Hurricanes are extra disruptive in part because the edge of the ocean is not a very safe place to live. Invasive species destroying native plants and trees come from careless human global transportation activities. Deer populations explode because we eliminate their natural predators and, in addition, stop eating them ourselves! Of course, many also argue that extreme weather events are becoming more frequent and more extreme because of changes in temperature that distort natural cycles, especially of moisture in the air. These changes are caused in large part by unfathomable amounts of carbon waste dumped into the atmosphere as a result of human activity.

A good deal of nature's apparent hostility is rooted in our desire to *dominate* nature, rather than learn its form. To dominate something (or someone) is to pay no attention to its own form, but rather only to how it can serve the desires of the master. Our desires are no longer shaped by a sense of wonder, care, and reverence for the existing creation. We no longer see God in the world. As we will see, Christian theology suggests that God has given humans a rightful "dominion" over nature, but we exercise that rule incorrectly, acting not in God's image and likeness, but according to our own wills. We might compare the difference between dominion and domination to the great and joyful challenge of parenting children. Parents do have "dominion" over their children, but they gravely harm relationships when they start to "dominate" their children. And so it is with us and the fabric of creation. When we lose the feeling of wonder in the face of the miraculous ordering of the world, we no longer understand our authority as limited by a higher power. Instead, we *are* the higher power.

Why does this happen? We will consider the problem in terms of three key spiritual diseases: scale, speed, and selfishness. These spiritual maladies are the underlying roots of our disruptive and disrupting relationship with the rest of creation, as well as with one another and our very selves. Attention to beauty and a recovery of the sense of wonder should help us see these diseases more clearly, for "once we are touched by beauty, we begin to notice the ways in which we need to be transformed."[2]

It's important to remember that problems with "the environment" are not new, not merely a product of our age. The history of human destruction of nature is a long one. Jared Diamond, in his book *Collapse*, provides fascinating (and chilling!) accounts of ancient civilizations that self-destructed because of abuses of the environment that were not recognized (or at least not acted upon!) until it was too late.[3] Our current condition has both similarities and differences to that of our ancestors. The same diseases can be seen in the ancient crises. But our situation is importantly different: the ancient problems were generally localized problems—they became a crisis more quickly but also limited the destructiveness of the crisis. Today, our scope is the entire globe.

This global scope of human domination is why the first disease we should look at is *scale*. We will come back again and again to scale, a spiritual temptation echoing the serpent's promise that we can be "like gods." What is meant by scale? Scale is an inescapable aspect of form. Consider an example: when we furnish a room, we ordinarily have some sense of whether items are the right size. While this sense of fit is not a precise science, we all understand that things can be too big or too small, disrupting the beauty of the scene. Similarly, humans participate in God's created order. But what is the correct scale of that participation? Humans are able to "think big"—as with so many of our abilities, this imagination is both a blessing and a curse.

In the introduction, we took a walk in part to appreciate this point about scale, about our relative size, and therefore our place in the order of things. That is why environmentalism so often emphasizes "small is beautiful," as E. F. Schumacher wrote in his environmental classic of the same name. Human spiritual problems often come from the illusions of our big thinking, otherwise known as the deadliest sin of pride. So too our environmental problems are rooted in our refusal to "think little," and work at an appropriate scale. "There is wisdom in smallness if only on account of the smallness and patchiness of human

knowledge. . . . The greatest danger invariably arises from the
ruthless application, on a vast scale, of partial knowledge."[4]
Nearly every practical problem we face today can be traced to
our inability to work at the right scale. Our houses, our farms,
our portion sizes are all too big. We put too much carbon into
the atmosphere, erode too much soil from our farms, use up
too much water, draw out too many fish—all these amazing
ecosystems can be used sustainably and can naturally renew
their "work" for human life, but only if we limit our scale. The
problem is not the things we are doing; the problem is that we
are doing too much of them.

The failure to work at an appropriate scale is usually related to mistakes about the purpose of our work. What do I
mean? Let us consider some examples of obviously overscaled
enterprises. We are all familiar with rich people and celebrities
building gaudy, oversized houses and throwing excessive parties. Why build a house so much bigger than necessary? Why
put so many resources to waste in a party? It seems impractical,
and it is. By impractical, we mean that the houses and parties
are no longer about their normal, practical purposes—shelter
and celebration with friends. All the excess? Its impractical
purpose is primarily shouting to the world about *themselves*.
The excess is about vanity competing with others who are vain,
in an "arms race" of excess on a virtually unlimited scale. Yet
aren't the rest of us often caught up in miniature versions of
these excessive choices?

The biblical tale of the tower of Babel is a classic spiritual
account of scale. "Come, let us build ourselves a city and a
tower with its top in the sky," the builders say, with a clearly
stated agenda to "make a name for ourselves" (Gen 11:4). It
is a vain project, a project not so much about a building, but
about the builders. God comes to see this project that human
"cooperation" is making possible, and says, "If now . . . they
have started to do this, nothing they presume to do will be out
of their reach" (Gen 11:6). They will do whatever their hearts
desire, however destructive and foolish. The last phrase is not

human's proper dominion, but rather human domination. God saves them from themselves by confusing their language, a confusion only reversed with the coming of the Holy Spirit on the disciples at Pentecost. The disciples can now speak to all, because they are no longer animated by vanity, no longer living for themselves.

Scale is a spiritual problem that goes back to an inability to see beauty. It is so focused on its own grand ambitions that it fails to not only the harm being caused but also the beauty of the order that actually exists and the need to work with that order. Perhaps the most Babel-like and absurd version of this illusion is in desert boom cities such as Las Vegas or the Middle Eastern oil center of Dubai. Las Vegas hotels construct elaborate displays of water (and do other water-intensive things like maintain golf courses), despite the region constantly living on the edge of a virtual water apocalypse, where the dropping level of the Lake Mead reservoir marks the impossibility of sustaining this project. Even more awash in wealth, generated by oil, Dubai is the kind of place where an enormous indoor ski mountain is built in the middle of a place where temperatures routinely top 110 degrees Fahrenheit (not to mention the world's tallest buildings, artificial lakes, and the like). These places are simply dramatic, stark examples of our general tendency to ignore the scale of given places in our desire to "make a name for ourselves."

Our second spiritual disease is *speed*. We are apt to lose any sense of beauty when we are moving too fast—passing through a landscape at highway speed (or flying over it!), or not settling down in a particular place and discovering its charms, or even not taking the time to prepare food properly. "Slow down and smell the flowers," we say. Speed is similar to the problem of scale but is applied to time. Since we cannot actually multiply hours in a day (we can build towers but are not godlike enough to command time!), we instead try to "make time" by doing things at greater and greater speed. In our day, we have coined the term "snail mail," applying it to delivery speeds that would have been seen as remarkably fast by those only a few generations ago. John O'Donohue points out that computer manufacturers "are constantly at work to cut the transition time" of the few seconds we spend waiting at "the vertical altar to go online." He writes, "We live under the imperative of the stand-alone digital instant"; thus, we become unable to understand the slow spiritual growth of ideas like journey and creativity, which are long, slow, and difficult.[5]

Theologian Norman Wirzba suggests that speed "drives and determines contemporary culture."[6] Though it is hard to believe, clocks are a relatively recent invention, and the standardization and exact measurement of time is a consequence of large-scale factory production and railroads. Being "on time" or even "ahead of schedule" is prized, as we "race with the clock." Today, it is not so much the clock or even the factory assembly line that sets the pace, but the revolution in time inaugurated by the internet. Media like Twitter and Vine flood us with ever-more-brief tidbits, and the wait of a few seconds for a download seems so long (compare this to the trip to a video store to rent the movie!). E-mails and, even more, Facebook demand constant updating. The whole system has been driven to even greater speeds once the internet became portable via smart phones. David Harvey characterizes the experience of our age as one of constant "time-space compression," processes that "alter, sometimes in quite radical ways, how we represent the world to ourselves." He quips that the end point of this process is when it gets "to the point where the present is all there is," which, according to modern psychology, is "the world of the schizophrenic."[7]

By contrast, Kelly Johnson reminds us that "God does not hurry," showing a patient trust especially in covenant fidelity. Unlike the supposedly godlike figures of the revolutionary or the superhero, who commit harm in order to achieve their goals, God has a great cause but also has "all the time in the world." Especially through Sabbath worship, God invites us to a much less hurried approach to life, one that shows "strange and disturbing patience."[8] At a recent Christmas Mass, I was pleasantly surprised to hear that Jesus' ancestry (Matt 1:1-17) was read rather than omitted (so we can *hurry* through Mass). The long trail of ancestry starting from Abraham indicates that God's plan, being born on that day, had taken *forty-two generations* to bring it to this point! Slow but sure.

God's slowness, like the slowness of natural processes, is apt to frustrate us if we allow our own desires to take charge. We'd like to speed up everything. Walking is just not very fast. Biking (a candidate for the most environmentally friendly invention of the modern era) still can't get us very far before we tire. Like no other invention, the automobile changed our physical environment, because we could go so far and so fast. Even the tiniest car engine packs the power of over a hundred horses; we command chariots that would have dwarfed those of Pharaoh.

Our obsession with speed creates many environmental problems, but it also goes further than that. It diminishes human community. As Wirzba points out, excessive speed "makes it much less likely that people will learn the disciplines of attention, conversation, and gratitude that are crucial in a celebratory and responsible life."[9] Haste makes waste, not just environmentally, but in terms of our community with others too. As is typical, the diseases that corrupt our natural ecology also corrupt our human ecology.

The final spiritual disease may seem more familiar: it is *selfishness*. But when I talk about selfishness here, I mean something peculiar to our time in history: the phenomenon called modern "individualism." People displaying selfishness is not new. However, for most of history, human beings understood their identity as constituted by their particular place in a social order, a social order that was in some sense related to the divine. That is, the order of the universe was reflected in the order of a society, where each person or family had their particular place. Life was experienced as rather fixed and stable, and one lived within given limits. People could be selfish in trying to take more than they were supposed to, but the whole definition of "supposed to" was enmeshed in relation to others and to the gods.

A few hundred years ago, discontent with the limits and abuses imposed by such orders led to the development of modern philosophies of individualism. In these philosophies, the social order was not sanctioned by some divine mandate but constructed (and reconstructed) by human beings. But for what purpose? Well, the most popular answer became for the mutual protection of individual rights, especially rights to life, liberty, and property. The social order was not fixed by God but rather something we could design to be useful for individuals, because it could secure our property, protect us from war and crime, and so forth.

Obviously, the rise of this way of understanding life in society brought many benefits. The Catholic tradition has noted how such societies can go to great lengths to defend "the dignity of the human person" and its link to "authentic freedom" (see *Gaudium et Spes* 12, 17). But as with scale and speed, it is possible for individualism to go to extremes. Rather than the individual serving the common good, we came to see society as simply a tool to serve whatever individuals wanted. It would not be far off to say that we flipped the traditional understanding on its head: instead of finding our place and identity in the social order, we used the social order to pursue our own desires and identity, whatever we willed them to be. Catholic philosopher Charles Taylor calls this "the great disembedding." As theologian Michael Northcott writes, "Modern individualism arises . . . from the distancing of self-consciousness from embodiment, and from the disembedding of the self from communities of place as traditionally constituted by the worship of God, and the correlative recognition of divine order in the cosmos and of divine intentionality in human society."[10]

As with scale and speed, we lost a sense of limits on the expansion of the self and our own desires. How can we grasp the kind of limits that exist when we think of ourselves first and foremost not as individuals, but as members of a team or group? Consider the most marketed-to groups in our society: teens, young adults, and seniors. We say these groups have "disposable income"—they are not the wealthiest groups, necessarily, but they are the groups whose spending (and whose lives) are not tied up and limited by the primary commitment of raising a family. In this case, "family" names a more traditional, fixed social order in which identity is wrapped up in the relationships. People are *embedded* in families. And this embedding works (though not always, of course!) to limit the expansion of desires of the self.

In the absence of vigorous forms of embedding, we face a peculiar sort of selfishness: a belief that we have "a right" to pursue our individual dreams, projects, and goals, so long as they don't hurt anyone else. In reality, human flourishing requires that we can situate our individual hopes and dreams, and our very selves, within a larger common order, what Catholic theology calls "the common good." Yet we are constantly preoccupied with freeing ourselves from any kind of decisive determination. Perhaps the greatest example of this is our ambivalence toward marriage, which appears to be the ultimate in staking oneself permanently to a common good. We continue to want it, but too often we want it only as long as we are "getting something out of it." Other traditional social relationships are also subtly and importantly changed to serve our individual rights and technological expansions—consider what "friendship" means on Facebook or what "following" means on Twitter. It is a world more and more revolving around and controlled by one person: me.

How does this particular sort of selfishness contribute to environmental problems? The connection is complex, and we will have to explore it more in our later chapters. But let's think about two examples where we treat individual desires as unquestioned. One is our personal consumption choices. Environmentalism often raises people's hackles because they resent others "telling them what to do." True, this can often be done in shrill and self-righteous ways, and sometimes without good reason. However, one thing we will confront head-on in this book is that living in harmony with the environment, if it is more than a nature poem on the wall, means understanding the profoundly *social* character of many of our everyday "life-style choices" and in particular their impact on our shared environment.

Another example is our tendency toward mobility, even within a single generation, much less over the course of generations. Genuine stewardship is most likely to happen when individuals and groups are committed to permanence in a particular place. This tends toward a careful appreciation of the place itself, but it also can redirect our time and energy toward more intangible, shared (and more environmentally friendly) activity. We become more interested in preservation and less interested in "what's new." We most especially develop a kind of knowledge that reflects an ability to see beauty. As Jame Schaefer notes, we also develop an appropriate "readiness to react negatively to ecological abuse,"[11] since we have developed a genuine affection for the place where we are and expect to remain.

Even within a region, our tendency to view house buying as a continual process of "trading up" has led to very environmentally destructive patterns of building and design. Typical American new homes today are over twice as large as new homes in the 1950s, and on larger lots, too, more remote from services and the central city. Meanwhile, those cities with developed cores, ones with neighborhoods where material sharing and common transportation are more possible, have often been allowed to decay and waste away, abandoned by those who might otherwise provide stability over time. No small portion of environmental overuse is caught up in this pattern of mobility.

In short, we sometimes assume that *to buy what we want* and *to move where we please* are simply individual rights. However, they may be dangerous manifestations of selfishness, manifestations that *collectively* produce a great deal of careless harm of creation.

Admittedly, new appliances or new home developments don't strike us as ugly. So we have to dig deeper to understand why these patterns are environmentally destructive. Let us literally "dig" to find the coal that energizes our homes and powers the factories in China that churn out the appliance. What does the process of getting this coal look like?

Coal has always competed for a spot at the absolute worst end of environmental villains, creating dangerous localized haze in so many industrializing centers, from nineteenth-century London to many cities in today's China (where coal is overwhelmingly the source of energy for the country's industrialization). Burning coal produces nearly twice as many greenhouse gases per energy unit as does using natural gas. The pollutants also contribute heavily to the problem of acid rain, which devastated forests in the Eastern United States—even after more stringent regulations, rain in eastern states remains significantly more acidic than normal.[12]

Coal pollutes the atmosphere . . . but what about getting the coal? Here, it is difficult to avoid the ugliness. Miners face potential disasters underground and potential diseases as they age. In the United States, all too often coal has proven to be one of the most devastatingly exploitative industries, leaving its main region chronically impoverished after many generations of "service" to "King Coal." (Despite this, one of the most exciting attractions of my childhood was descending into the "working coal mine" at Chicago's Museum of Science and Industry! I do not recall any concerns being raised in that exhibit.)

With the help of heavy machinery developed for World War II, companies increasingly turned to "strip mining," which "produces many more tons of coal per worker hour" but is "more destructive," since "the landscape is literally stripped away—including trees and soil—in order to access a layer of coal beneath."[13] While backlash prompted legislation for subsequent "reclamation" of the land, such regulations are often ignored or skirted.

Strip mining has now been "topped" by the current state-of-the-art practice in coal mining, called, "mountaintop removal mining." It is exactly what it sounds like. As the EPA, in studiedly neutral language, describes it, "Mountaintop coal mining is a surface mining practice involving the removal of

mountaintops to expose coal seams, and disposing of the associated mining overburden in adjacent valleys—'valley fills.'"
The process involves stripping what is termed as "overburden" (i.e., the forest and natural soils) to expose coal seams, dumping the overburden into nearby valleys, often covering miles of streams. The EPA estimates "Appalachian coal mining has buried an estimated 2,000 miles of streams in states including West Virginia."[14] Later, after the "spoil" (the coal) is taken, the area is "regraded" and "revegetated." Theoretically, the 1977 Surface Mining Control and Reclamation Act requires companies to restore land to the "general surface configuration of the land prior to mining," including its "approximate original contour," but these regulations are ignored.[15]

The EPA's site provides pictures of this process. They are not pretty.[16] In fact, anyone flying west into or out of the Washington, DC, area is likely to see these massive operations as gaping gray sores. The scale is much larger than strip mining, which could only access coal several feet below the surface. Mountaintop removal operations can go as far as 1,000 feet deep. One proposed operation the EPA considered (and ultimately rejected in 2011) would have cleared 2,200 acres of "mature, productive forestlands" and buried over seven miles of pristine stream habitat.[17] Needless to say, the process involves massive heavy equipment and explosives. One resident of a West Virginia town said that when blasting started, "you could wash your car today, and tomorrow you could write your name on it in the dust," and the mining company decided it was better to buy out the entire town and bulldoze it, rather than "deal with all the complaint-generated inspections, or the possible lawsuits over silica dust and 'fly rock.' "[18] It is unsurprising that residents of well-off areas would violently oppose such projects on many grounds, but sadly, the reality of areas of West Virginia and Kentucky where these projects predominate is economically so depressed that it is tolerated. Moreover, this area faces stiff competition from the now-dominant surface mines in Wyoming, which produces more than twice as much coal as West Virginia.

Even allowing mountaintop removal may not "save jobs" in this area; a recent *Wall Street Journal* article noted that the industry is "consolidating," and that areas in the East are in "decline" as "coal production plunges" compared to "open-pit mines in Wyoming and under the plains of Illinois and Indiana."[19] These mines have their own environmental problems, but surely the image of blasting off and flattening the tops of ancient forested mountains constitutes a kind of pinnacle of human hubris.

Why discuss this? It's important to know that, as we will see later in the text, our oversized appetites for food and energy drive these processes. There are, of course, other and much more environmentally careful ways to extract fuel, but they are considerably more costly—a situation that might lead to leaving the coal in the ground and opting for other energy sources, or simply push us to be smarter about conserving energy. We could still have energy, but we'd have less of it. What is certain: if we did not do this, energy costs will be higher, and we believe this to be intolerable. Cheap energy and its products are apparently worth sacrificing mountains.

This example is clearly a case of human evil despoiling nature. Unlike our farmer managing a pesky deer population, mountaintop removal is not a solution to a real tension in nature. It is not a matter of ecological balance that simply appears "violent" *from our perspective*. Instead, mountaintop removal is an example of our temptations to unlimited scale, speed, and selfishness. Carolyn Merchant writes that, prior to modernity, when spiritual traditions had a stronger sense of the earth as living, the tendency to image the earth as feminine (e.g., "mother earth") meant that both classical and Christian writers viewed the very activity of mining as highly suspect, a kind of "invasive assault."[20] The more we delight in nature's beauty, the more destruction like this should disturb us spiritually.

So why, if we do delight in nature's beauty, do we also engage in such ugliness? In this chapter, I have suggested part of the problem is a kind of counterspirituality, preoccupied with scale, speed, and the maximum satisfaction of our desires. This counterspirituality means that we find cooperation with nature's form to be at best slow, and at worst demanding and downright unpleasant. We eschew careful work for other gratifications. We demand the world meet our specifications. This counter-spirituality informs a cultural desire for things like abortion, divorce on demand, euthanasia, drugs of all sorts. It is corrosive to relationships of fidelity, trust, and compassion. But we make a mistake if we don't see that the same counter-spirituality is at work when we tolerate and benefit from environmental destruction. As Christians, it is the same story—the same set of biblical beliefs about God's story of creation and salvation—that underlies our concern for all these issues. We turn to the specifics of that story, and their key implications for the environment, in the next two chapters.

chapter 3

Basic Theology I
Creation and Covenant

The created world, structured in an intelligent way by God, is entrusted to our responsibility, and though we are able to analyze it and transform it, we cannot consider ourselves creation's absolute master.

—Benedict XVI[1]

Our initial chapters focused on what might be called a "spirituality of the environment," a way of attuning our sentiments, attitudes, and vision to see nature well. In the next two chapters, we'll look at the specific theological commitments of Christianity in order to provide a clear foundation for these spiritual insights, and to give them more sharpness and precision. In Catholicism, the environment does not always get the attention it deserves, especially compared to other topics of public, moral concern. This is unfortunate especially because the basic principles that support Catholic teaching on the environment—such as God's sovereignty over all creation, God's salvific will for all creatures, and the human need for restraint—are the same ones that support many other key Catholic positions on issues like abortion, artificial reproductive technologies, and euthanasia. Pope Benedict XVI has pointedly made this connection by stating, "The book of nature is one and indivisible: it takes in not only the environment but also life, sexuality, marriage, the family, social relations. . . . Our duties toward the environment are linked to our duties toward the human person. . . . It would be wrong to uphold one set of duties while trampling on the other" (*Caritas in Veritate* 51).

The obvious foundation for Catholic environmentalism is the Christian belief about creation, rooted in Hebrew tradition: creation is entirely good, and all of it comes from God. The US bishops' statement on the environment begins with this view: "The heavens and the earth, the sun and the moon, the earth and the sea, fish and birds, animals and humans—all are good. God's wisdom and power were present in every aspect of the unfolding of creation."[2] This is the bedrock. Pope Benedict writes, "In nature, the believer recognizes the wonderful result of God's creative activity, which we may use responsibly to satisfy our legitimate needs, while respecting the intrinsic balance of creation." Creation has a balance, a "design of love and truth," an "inbuilt order" (*Caritas in Veritate* 48). Respecting this balance is respecting God's wisdom and power as Creator.

In this chapter, we will develop this idea of God as Creator, with a particular focus on the Old Testament. In it, we find the familiar creation story, but also the less familiar (to most of us) stories of God's covenant relationship with God's people, Israel. The creation story itself is rooted in this ongoing covenant relationship—a relationship that is in no way purely "spiritual" or "individual." Within a common life of holiness and love structured by God's law, the covenant is "a fundamentally interactive account of the relations between the human self, the social order and natural ecological order, and between all of these and the being of God."[3] This story of the covenant is meant to act as a contrast, the story of a "contrast-society" from its roots in the liberation from Egypt to its darkest days in exile. It is a story of God's long, slow work to bring us back from sin. The teachings of the covenant remain a challenging contrast to some of our prevalent cultural beliefs and practices today. In chapter 4, I will turn to the story of redemption in Christ, but it is always important to recognize that the early church intentionally adopted the Hebrew Scriptures as genuinely Christian Scripture. It does not reveal some different "Old Testament God"; it reveals the *same God* that appears in the New Testament. The church rejected the attempt by Marcion, in the second century, to exclude the Old Testament from the canon. Yet we are constantly tempted by the heresy of Marcionism when we ignore creation and covenant as a continuing foundation for the Christian life.

Let us appreciate the stories of creation first. The story of the seven days in Genesis 1 is best seen as a theological poem, not a scientific account, which depicts the careful work of God in creating all the world through acts of speaking. Not only is the text a poem, but God works like a poet, through speaking! Biblical scholars have long noted the contrast between this way of depicting God's creation with the stories of other traditions surrounding Israel in ancient times. Most common in those other narratives, creation is described as the result of some kind of conflict and violence among the gods, or as something wrestled from chaos by the conquering strength of the gods. Michael Northcott highlights a common contrast with the Sumerian creation myth, where the warrior Marduk creates the world from "killing, trampling and then splitting open the body of the goddess Tiamat, and he fashions humans from the dead body of Tiamat's consort Kingu." Notice the message of these other creation myths: "Reality is fundamentally chaotic, and order only attainable through violence."[4]

By contrast, Genesis 1 presents us with an entirely peaceful picture, with absolutely no sense of conflict. Even in the (older) story of Genesis 2, God fashions the human (*adam* is the Hebrew word) as a potter from soil (*adamah* is the word for soil; Gen 2:7)—hence, the human is presented as "soil creature"! Extending the nonviolent imagery, God even puts the human "under anesthesia," as it were, for the rib transplant that brings forth woman. To say creation is peaceful is to say that, according to God's intentions, all the parts work together as one harmonious whole. Violence is not required to create.

Several other elements of the creation stories should be noted. One is the unique balance they achieve in distinguishing God from the creation and yet not rendering the creation as somehow a "fall" from God. Creation is *neither* divine *nor* somehow flawed or subpar; rather, it is simply good as it is. Thus, on the one hand, these stories reject any kind of worship of nature or natural features. They do not accord a special divine place to a particular tree or animal, to the sun or the moon. All of these are from God. All too often, making certain things sacred can lead to the destruction of whatever is "not sacred." But on the other hand, the story rejects any kind of dualism, which suggests the material world is somehow bad or disordered in itself. What we call "sin" *only enters the picture later* and is not part of the original creation. The nondivine character of creation doesn't mean inferiority or defect. The relentless refrain of the poem, "God saw that it was good"—notice the seeing!—suggests that the entire natural order reflects the divine wisdom, though it is not divine itself. Another feature to notice: God is depicted as dividing day from night, sea from land, sun from moon—but not to say "one is good, the other is bad" or "day is better than night." Rather, the division creates a harmony, a harmony that culminates in the simultaneous creation of humans as male and female.

The next key feature of the creation story is the statement that humans are made "in God's image." We have probably heard this many times; remember that it is meant to be a striking claim. What exactly does it mean? Ellen Davis explains that the *imago Dei* is oriented to a "mastery" that involves securing the food system, as explained in some detail in Genesis 1:29-30: "Behold, I have given you every plant yielding seed which is upon the face of all the earth, and every tree with seed in its fruit; you shall have them for food. And to every beast of the earth, and to every bird of the air, and to everything that creeps on the earth, everything that has the breath of life, I have given every green plant for food." Davis notes that its presence here indicates being in the image of God means "recognizing and perpetuating the sufficiency God has provided."[5] Pope Benedict reiterates this idea, saying that nature's order enables humans "to draw from it the principles to till it and keep it" (*Caritas in Veritate* 48). Thus, agricultural responsibility is the first aspect of the *imago Dei*! While God concedes meat eating to Noah (Gen 9:3-5), and the creation story authors were well aware that many animals are carnivores, this behavior apparently does not reflect the original wisdom of God—much as patriarchy, accepted throughout the Bible, is a concession that is not in accord with God's design of original equality of the sexes.

This command of dominion over the earth has been commonly misinterpreted. To "subdue the earth" was taken to mean that all creation was to be used by humans as they saw fit, as if the divine order could be completely changed by us. E. F. Schumacher writes of the effects of this misinterpretation: "Modern man does not experience himself as a part of nature but as an outside force destined to dominate and conquer it."[6] Indeed, Davis herself notes the Hebrew verb here is most like "to conquer"—what the Israelites did to other peoples as they took possession of the Promised Land.[7] Yet if we are disturbed by the Old Testament "conquest" stories (as we usually are!), we should also be disturbed by the idea that God accepts or even encourages our violent "conquest" of nature, simply giving everything to humans to do whatever they want with it. Such a message would stand in stark contrast to the rest of the Bible!

Rather than misinterpreting dominion as domination, the idea is better understood as an ultimate subordination to God's purposes. As Northcott explains, "The Hebrew root of the verb translated subdue or rule means vice-regent or steward and not ruler. God puts humans over nature not as owner or exploiter but as the steward who shares the creative care of the creator."[8] Davis reminds us that Israel's "conquering" of the Promised Land is *not* so they can do whatever they want, but so that they can live according to God's law. Thus, it established the land as ultimately belonging to God, not to the Israelites for their own selfish purposes.[9] Hence (as we shall see), God's extensive, detailed provisions for *how* Israelites are to use the land. The most important? The prohibition of complete domination in the form of absolute ownership of the land!

Most important, Northcott suggests that dominion involves a respect for all living things *on their own terms*—much as the beekeeper Kirk Webster, whom we met earlier, learns the ways of the bees. God's very creation is a making room for all of creation to be. As the psalms suggest, the ultimate destiny of all things (not just humans) is to glorify God:

> Praise him, sun and moon;
> > praise him, all shining stars.
> Praise him, highest heavens,
> > you waters above the heavens. . . .
> Praise the LORD from the earth,
> > you sea monsters and all the deeps of the sea;
> Lightning and hail, snow and thick clouds,
> > storm wind that fulfills his command;
> Mountains and all hills,
> > fruit trees and all cedars;
> Animals wild and tame,
> > creatures that crawl and birds that fly . . .
> Let them all praise the LORD's name . . . (Ps 148:3-4, 7-10, 13)

What a litany of creation! All of these are established by God and ordered to his praise. They have a God-given integrity that should not be violated, even as they are used. A similar kind of respectful care can be seen in the Genesis 2 story of the human *naming* the animals. To know someone's name is, in the Old Testament as today, to signal respect, to affirm one's identity as equal to others. To say "Hey, you" or "Yes, sir" is to imply an unequal relationship. But people we know, animals we name, even natural features that we name—these are what we tend to treat with real care. Nameless people or animals or places are sadly more apt to be treated harshly.

The creation story concludes with the Sabbath, which Norman Wirzba calls "the climax of creation" and "the model for what our life together in a place should look like."[10] It is not just a rest stop, a "reprieve in the midst of an otherwise frantic or obsessive life." It is when "creation becomes what it fully ought to be," achieving what Rabbi Abraham Heschel called a "conscious harmony" of humans, the world, and God.[11] It is the *completion* of work, not exhaustion *from* it. Hence, Sabbath living is not an invitation to "luxurious ease" but rather a matter of being "fully present" and practicing "the attention and practical discipline that enables us to know deeply who we are and who we are with."[12] Famously, Karl Barth suggested that the Sabbath rest was meant to orient work, reminding us we "must work in all seriousness" but never prioritize work in a way that surpasses God's ordering, never "believing in [our] work" to such an extent that it becomes a rival to God's wisdom of original ordering.[13] Keeping a Sabbath is perhaps the most concrete way to show our self-restraint in work.

From the creation story, then, we learn that humans have a privileged place in creation, but it is a place *within* a carefully established divine order. They have privileges, but with those privileges they bear responsibilities for nurturing this order, "tending" it as one does to a garden or a flock of sheep. The created world is not just raw material. Human responsibility can also mean human failure, of course—as we see in the stories of sin that immediately follow in Genesis. It is not insignificant to note that in the flood God saves all the animals along with Noah's family!

The fall into sin unleashes disorder not only within humans (what Catholics call concupiscence) and among them (injustice) but also within the entire natural order. The fall is "cosmic" in this sense, just as the redemption restores order not just to humans but to the entirety of creation. In terms of the environment, we can think of the fall as a refusal to acknowledge creaturehood in our responsibilities to act as stewards of God's creation. Pope Benedict writes, "Conflict arose within and between [hu]mankind and the rest of creation. Human beings let themselves be mastered by selfishness; they misunderstood the meaning of God's command and exploited creation out of a desire to exercise absolute dominion over it."[14] We become "like gods" in the bad sense, becoming tyrannical, ruthless rulers instead of being "like God" in the originally intended way!

Here, let us recall our comments earlier about so-called "natural evil." The conflicts and danger we experience from natural forces are mysteriously wrapped up in the human rebellion against creaturehood, against being creatures of a good God who has designed creation in a good way. While it is not appropriate to attribute particular natural events to God's direct action, it is quite biblical to suggest that experiences of "the wrath of nature" can be discerned in general as a kind of judgment, a kind of "wages of sin," whereby we are brought to consider the effects of our lack of humility. God is not really like a magical computer programmer or a puppeteer, pulling strings and punching buttons to produce natural events. However, God is willing (as in the exile from the Garden of Eden) to let the processes of nature carry a kind of tension, a kind of pain and danger to us, that is the result of human sin.

It would be absolutely terrible to stop here, though! Despite humanity's fall into sin, God does not leave us. God persists in his desire to save creation, unfolding a plan that centers on the formation of a special people, Israel, forming a special *covenant* with them. The central feature of that covenant is an *extended law*. Christians often mistakenly believe that the law is set up as a kind of test, a final exam for the afterlife. But even a brief perusal of the law shows that its contents don't really fit this interpretation. Consider this example, from the chapter following the Ten Commandments: "When men quarrel and one strikes the other with a stone or with his fist, not mortally, but enough to put him in bed, the one who struck the blow shall be acquitted, provided the other can get up and walk around with the help of his staff. Still, he must compensate him for his recovery time and make provision for his complete healing" (Exod 21:18-19). Or another: "When one man's ox hurts another's ox and it dies, they shall sell the live ox and divide this money as well as the dead animal equally between them. But if it was known that the ox was previously in the habit of goring and its owner would not watch it, he must make full restitution, an ox for an ox; but the dead animal he may keep" (Exod 21:35-36). Just continue this part of Exodus for many more examples!

If the law is not given as an afterlife exam, what is its purpose? It is to guide Israel to become a light to the nations, to display *in practice* to a fallen world what it might look like for people to live according to God's will for the world, rather than simply for themselves. The words of Torah are the path to reestablishing God's harmonious ordering. We are most familiar with the Ten Commandments, the basic rules outlining relationships with God and with others. But the law does not stop there—rabbis count 613 laws in the Old Testament covenant, which cover in extraordinary detail the conduct of the community.

The law has a great deal to say about the environment. Much stealing, lying, and even killing goes on in environmentally destructive activity. But let us consider an even deeper message: Ellen Davis calls the often-neglected legal codes of Exodus, Leviticus, and Deuteronomy the place where we find "the most detailed scriptural witness regarding how we might live within the intended harmony of God's creation," offering an overall vision of "wholesome materiality."[15] The law as a whole is an approach to *material* life that places it within the whole life of the people oriented to God. It makes our handling of the material into a profoundly spiritual vocation. As we will see, it is quite similar to what Catholics mean when they talk about the "sacramental" character of the material world. This approach rejects any kind of dualism of the material and the spiritual, as if somehow "spiritual things" are a separate realm of their own. The use of the material creation is a spiritual act, since creation is an order received from and presided over by God, with human use directed by God's law.

We may have an unfortunate stereotype of Old Testament law as prescribing lots of seemingly meaningless ritual. In fact, the law's "wholesome materiality" is much more focused on how animals and the land are to be treated. There is no supposed authority to "dominate" animals and the land indiscriminately. On the contrary, *restrained* use is the chief theme. For example, the law enjoins certain kinds of treatment of animals, which, as Northcott notes, are not a matter of "animal rights" but rather a recognition that animals share "in the divine-inspired character of all of life."[16] Even the slaughter regulations are more humane than the conventional practices of the time—and often more humane than our contemporary meat factories! Furthermore, it is telling that the common practice of animal sacrifice is increasingly frowned upon as the text develops. God insists that "I desire steadfast love [mercy], and not sacrifice; the knowledge of God, rather than burnt offerings" (Hos 6:6, RSV; cf. Matt 12:7). In the prophet Amos, God rages,

> I hate, I despise your feasts,
>> I take no pleasure in your solemnities.
> Even though you bring me your burnt offerings and grain offerings
>> I will not accept them;
> Your stall-fed communion offerings,
>> I will not look upon them. . . .
> Rather let justice surge like waters,
>> and righteousness like an unfailing stream.
>> (Amos 5:21-22, 24)

In the prophet Isaiah, God says,

> What do I care for the multitude of your sacrifices?
>> says the LORD.
> I have had enough of whole-burnt rams
>> and fat of fatlings;
> In the blood of calves, lambs, and goats
>> I find no pleasure. . . .
>> [C]ease doing evil;
>> learn to do good.
> Make justice your aim: redress the wronged,
>> hear the orphan's plea, defend the widow. (Isa 1:11, 16-17)

Certainly the ceasing of animal sacrifices is good for animals!

A second, even more important example of the ecological bent of the law concerns the *many* rules and restrictions placed on land use. Significantly, a "Sabbath" for the land is insisted upon, so that its fertility might not be exhausted. This Sabbath does not merely honor God but is explicitly "for the land" itself.[17] There are also a whole host of rules that, combined with the law prohibiting lending at interest, are designed to make it nearly impossible to accumulate large amounts of land and hold them indefinitely. Land may be leased out but is then returned to the ancestral tribe.

We may have a difficult time understanding why God is so interested in controlling real estate transactions. The answer is clearly ecological: since land cannot be bought and sold outright, nor loans acquired to accumulate large amounts of land, the quick accumulation of vast wealth through the exploitation and exhaustion of land is made impossible. This is a case of limiting *scale*. As Northcott writes, "According to the [later] Hebrew prophets the land turned to desert not when it was farmed equitably by ancestral groups but when it was inequitably acquired for the commercial gain and greed of the rich. Land is part of the covenant community . . . and through the covenant character of land moral duties are established in the Torah in relation to the whole biosphere. . . . The welfare and goods of human society are set in the context of the welfare and goods of the covenanted cosmos."[18] Walter Brueggemann notes that even the major commandments against coveting have specific concerns—the neighbor's *wife* and *fields*. Why these? Not for psychological reasons, but in order to limit selfish accumulations of fertility.[19]

This concern to limit and order material behavior is central even beyond the law itself. The first stories of Israel after their liberation from Egypt reflect this same kind of ecological concern. No sooner are they freed than the Israelites start "grumbling," anxious about food for their desert trek and pining for "Egypt, as we sat by our kettles of meat and ate our fill of bread!" (Exod 16:3). This grumbling leads God to send manna, in order that the Israelites might further trust in God's providence and protection. However, there are rules attached to manna collection: there is to be *no gathering on the Sabbath* (Exod 16:25-27), and there is to be *no storing of surplus* (Exod 16:16-20); households should take what they need for the day, and no more. As Davis notes, these rules make food "the litmus test of Israel's separation from the culture and mind-set of Egypt"—contrasting trust in human work of accumulating and hoarding surplus with a trust in the goodness of God.[20] Thus, in regard to food as the ultimate sign of material possession, "Israel is called upon to engage in two concrete practices of restraint, namely, eschewing excess and keeping Sabbath."[21] Both God and Moses are angry when some in the camp disobey both rules, taking excess (which miraculously rots overnight!) and going out to gather on the Sabbath. The rules for manna are a way of practicing ecological restraint through economic modesty. They are mirrored and echoed in Jesus' prayer to God for "our daily bread" (Matt 6:11) and his admonition not to worry about food (Matt 6:25).

As the Old Testament proceeds, it becomes clear that social disorder and ecological disaster go together, and they both happen when Israelites get greedy, wanting to be "like the nations" and skirting the law. We are used to hearing how God "hears the cry of the poor" and how Israel's prophets rail against the rich, such as Amos:

> [T]hey hand over the just for silver,
>   and the poor for a pair of sandals;
> They trample the heads of the destitute
>   into the dust of the earth,
>   and force the lowly out of the way. (2:6-7)

However, the desolation of the land itself is also a prominent theme in the prophetic literature. The Chronicler recounts the exile, saying, "All this was to fulfill the word of the Lord spoken by Jeremiah: Until the land has retrieved its lost sabbaths, during all the time it lies waste it shall have rest while seventy years are fulfilled" (2 Chr 36:21).

In all, much of what the law is designed to do is place limits on human temptations to sinfulness and disorder. For example, the famous commandment "an eye for an eye" (Exod 21:24) is an attempt to *limit* the violence of vengeance. All too often, when we are hurt by others, we want to hurt them back—*a lot more* than they hurt us! Similarly, juridical laws governing conflict, marriage, slavery, even stray oxen consistently limit and curtail possible open-ended conflict. Even the great commandment against stealing, Robert Gnuse argues, is not about petty theft but "to curb those who steal from society at large by amassing great wealth, for such theft will ultimately break down that society."[22] As we will see in later chapters, key environmental limits are set by laws limiting (1) land accumulation and (2) money accumulation through lending at interest, or usury. Each of these places a limit on human greed that, when ignored, develops into the potential for enormous environmental exploitation.

The law is not just about limits. The limits serve its central ideal that "you shall love your neighbor as yourself" (Lev 19:18), promoting special care for the orphan, the widow, and the alien. In this very chapter of Leviticus, the landowner is commanded, "When you reap the harvest of your land, you shall not be so thorough that you reap the field to its very edge, nor shall you gather the gleanings of your harvest," for these are to be left "for the poor and the alien" (Lev 19:9, 10). In particular, the "alien" should be protected "no differently than the natives born among you; you shall love the alien as yourself; for you too were once aliens in the land of Egypt" (Lev 19:34). In an age where so much of America's food is harvested by migrant workers denigrated as "aliens," this is also a message we need to heed! Thus, in its treatment of humans, animals, and land, the law offers more than just limits on sin: it is a path toward restoring the harmony of the creation by using creation's gifts as a sign of generosity and human communion. Catholics need to consider carefully how we may have lost sight of many aspects of this vision of creation and covenant. In particular, the keeping of Sabbath, the just treatment of animals, and the limits on absolute land ownership all contest our obsessions with scale, speed, and selfish individualism in maximizing our accumulation of property, regardless of the effects on community. These tenets of the law are all affirmed today in the *Catechism of the Catholic Church*. But the Catechism's story also goes further, as does the Bible's. It goes to the fullness of God's work in Jesus. We must learn next how our misunderstanding of the significance of Jesus' person and work is rooted in our inability to see him as completing this long story of covenant. It is to the New Testament completion that we now turn.

chapter 4

Basic Theology II
Redemption and Renewal

The justified concern about threats to the environment present in so many parts of the world is reinforced by Christian hope, which commits us to working responsibly for the protection of creation. The relationship between the Eucharist and the cosmos helps us to see the unity of God's plan and to grasp the profound relationship between creation and the "new creation" inaugurated in the resurrection of Christ, the new Adam.

—Benedict XVI[1]

In 1967, Lynn White (a Christian) wrote one of the most famous articles in the history of the environmental movement. In it, he accused the Christian tradition of standing at the "historical roots of the ecological crisis."[2] Why? White suggested a fatal combination of two factors: the Genesis command to dominate and subdue the earth, and a preoccupation with an otherworldly picture of individual soul salvation. These together led Christians to view the creation as mere raw material, with no significance other than as means to achieve purely spiritualized goals. In the last chapter, we primarily studied the story of the Old Testament in order to overcome the first mistake. We learned that

41

humanity's dominion is not domination but is properly named by the rules of restraint and care found in the covenant law. In this chapter, we explore the other end of White's critique. If Christianity is in fact a spiritual religion concerned with individual soul salvation, does caring for creation ultimately matter?

In order to answer this question well, we need to explore three other questions. First, what exactly does "salvation" or "redemption" mean? Second, how does Catholicism see the sacraments as essential for salvation? And third, why does Jesus offer such a harsh critique of riches and possessions? From these three threads, we can weave a truly Catholic theology of the environment that goes beyond just saying, "God created the world and saw that it was good."

Let's begin at the end: what is the goal of the Christian life? Theology calls this "eschatology," the doctrines about the last things. Everyone recognizes that the goal has to do with "salvation"—the name Jesus means "God saves"—but what exactly this means and *what it requires of us* have been a topic of Christian theological debate from the very beginning. In the book of Acts, the church's first "council" of leaders at Jerusalem involves the salvation question: Do non-Jewish converts to Jesus' way have to obey all of Old Testament law, particularly about circumcision (something an adult convert might want to avoid!)? The conclusion? Basically, keep "only a couple important parts," namely, "to avoid pollution from idols, unlawful marriage, the meat of strangled animals, and blood" (Acts 15:20).

The point of the Acts story is not to offer a definitive list of individual hoops. Instead, it's important to see the continuity from Old to New Testament. The question of salvation is the question of how to be part of God's covenant community. Just as in the Old Testament, from the very beginning, "being saved" is essentially linked to *becoming a part of the church*, of God's people. As Pope Benedict stressed in his encyclical *Spe Salvi*, salvation is *social*. He cautions against a "pure individualism" of salvation and insists that "salvation has always been considered a 'social' reality" (*Spe Salvi* 13–14). As Benedict writes, "Sin is

understood by the [church] Fathers as the destruction of the
unity of the human race. . . . Hence, redemption appears as the
re-establishment of unity in which we come together once more
in a union that begins to take place in the world community of
believers" (ibid., 14). When Christians profess their baptismal
promises, the beliefs are not just about God and the story of
what happened to Jesus. Christians also believe in "the holy
catholic Church, the communion of saints, the forgiveness of
sins, the resurrection of the body, and life everlasting." Thus,
"salvation" involves being bodily joined to God's people, who
are themselves the Body of Christ, the new Adam of the new
creation. To become a part of this Body, we pass through the Red
Sea of baptism and celebrate the Lord's Supper with our new
family in the "Promised Land." Eternal life, Benedict says, "is
linked to a lived union with a 'people,' and for each individual
it can only be attained within this *we*" (ibid.).

Notice how *material* all this is. We can easily miss this if we
start thinking it is all an elaborate (and confusing!) metaphor
for having a private relationship with God in our soul. It's not.
Instead, it really is a bodily entrance into the corporate Body
that constitutes our initiation into the new creation. In this new
Spirit-filled community, we as individuals take our place and find
our specific missions and use our different gifts for the purposes
of God's kingdom. This brief story sums up not only the New
Testament but also the basic doctrines of the Christian creed
and the central ritual life of the church's sacraments.

Once we see this, we might be shaken free of a different
dominant image of "salvation": our souls getting to heaven
when we die. This image is certainly true, but it can become
too central to our faith. The primary focus of the Christian story
is instead the gathering of the people of the new creation from
every corner of the earth, a creation in Christ that even the
world's powers of death cannot destroy. (Hence, we should be
willing to risk even our lives for it, knowing that God will raise
us up—that's where the heaven part is supposed to come in!)
Benedict reminds us that "this community-oriented vision of

the blessed life is certainly directed beyond this present world"
but "it also has to do with the building up of this world" (*Spe
Salvi* 15). This new creation is already happening, even if it is
not yet complete. Salvation is our life becoming a part of this
thing that will endure forever.

Three biblical images need to be highlighted here that best
represent to us what Christians hope for "in the end." One is
the city, the heavenly Jerusalem—we will discuss this image in
a later chapter when we turn to the question of how we think
about our built environment and its impact on the earth. Another is the marriage of "the new heavens and new earth," also
explained as the marriage of Christ and the church. The Catechism indicates this is the truly final reality—"after heaven,"
you might say—and indicates firmly that this vision "affirms the
profound common destiny of the material world and [human-
kind]" such that "the visible universe" is "transformed" and
"restored to its original state."[3] Finally, there is the frequent
image of the banquet, the feast, which can be tied into the
image of the wedding. So what we get is something like a whole
community getting together for a massive wedding celebration.
Perhaps this is what a society does for a royal wedding. Besides
being communal, these images are resolutely material. They
suggest the real promise of redemption involves new creation.

All of this leads to our first, most basic point about Christian
salvation and the earth: the proper end goal of Christianity is
not escape from creation, but hope for a radical renewal of it.
We pray for this every time we speak the Our Father. We do not
ask God to get us to heaven, but rather that "thy kingdom come"
and God's "will be done *on earth* as it is in heaven." As God says
in the book of Revelation, "Behold, I make all things new" (Rev
21:5)—and not "Behold, I make a new set of things." Vatican II
insists that "far from diminishing our concern to develop this
earth, the expectancy of a new earth should spur us on, for it is
here that the body of a new human family grows." The present
world passes away only insofar as it is "distorted by sin" (*Catechism* 1049, 1048; quoting *Gaudium et Spes* 39).

Thus, White's critique of Christianity's account of salvation as leading to the neglect of creation really only applies to a *distorted, partial form* of Christianity, although one that is unfortunately too common in its history. Indeed, from its very beginnings, Christianity has been tempted by a heresy that gained the name of "Gnosticism"—that salvation involves some kind of special knowledge by which our souls can escape from the material prison of this world and be with the divine. One form of this was the second-century proposal of Marcion to reject the entire Old Testament, on the grounds that Jesus had revealed the true, "spiritual" God. This was rejected by the early church. At its extreme, Gnostic forms of Christianity suggest the whole of material creation is the result of a "fall" from a spiritual state, an image obviously contrary to the Genesis stories. Gnosticism also tends to have a difficult time acknowledging the "truly human" part of the incarnation of Christ, especially Jesus' death. How could God really become flesh? Gnostic forms of Christianity often reveal themselves through images of a kind of "Superman-Jesus"—like Superman, Clark Kent *appears* to be human, but really it is only an appearance; Jesus' flesh is more like a disguise than a genuine sanctification.

In response, Christianity has from the very beginning affirmed not only that creation is from God and all good but that what we need to be "saved" from is *sin*, not material creation. We need to be liberated from the distorted patterns that the Gospel of John calls "the world." Our escape is not from God's good material order, but rather from our enslavement to sin, to the powers of distortion and distraction. The great opponent of second-century Gnosticism, St. Irenaeus, argues above all for "the unity of God's creative and redemptive purposes for the created order and for embodied human life, and the self-in-relation, as part of that order."[4] "Creation shows its Creator," says Irenaeus, "and what is made suggest its Maker."[5] Christ is "recapitulating all things in Himself," finishing creation as we have matured through salvation history (cf. Eph 1:10).[6] Once we are able to see this, Catholic ecological mission should be strengthened, not weakened—

because we are saved from a common despair that environmental change is impossible! For "what is impossible for human beings is possible for God" (Luke 18:27).

Having recognized that salvation involves a renewal and transformation of creation, rather than an escape from it, we can move to our second point: we learn the full meaning and true materiality of our redemption by participating in the "new world" that is opened up by the practices we call *sacraments*. As the US bishops point out in their earliest letter on the environment, we live in a "sacramental universe" and that "for many people, the environmental movement has reawakened appreciation of the truth that, through the created gifts of nature, men and women encounter their Creator."[7] This sacramental worldview means that God and humanity become joined *in and through the material world*—not invisibly, not in some pure interior solitude, but in the water, the bread, the oil, the laying on of hands. As the psalmist exclaims,

> Taste and see that the LORD is good;
> blessed is the stalwart one who takes refuge in him. (Ps 34:9)

Sometimes the sacraments can seem cut off from the material world. There is an important point being made here: the transformation from creation to new creation is not "just there" and apparent everywhere. It is a process, which requires us to discern where and how God is manifest in a creation that is still mixed with sin. The sacraments are a kind of special form that train us to see in this way; one author properly calls them a "dress rehearsal," where we learn the whole of the play very intently so that we can go out and perform it.[8] As with our recognition of beauty, learning the form of the new creation does take special attention.

But it is certainly true that the separation of the sacraments from the rest of life can go too far. In one of the most famous phrases from the Vatican II Constitution on the Sacred Liturgy, the liturgy is called "the source and summit of the Christian life" (*Sacrosanctum Concilium* 10). This saying emphasizes the absolutely central importance of sacramental liturgies—but its importance as understood in connection to and as orientation for the entirety of our lives. This doesn't simply mean making the hour at Mass your "can't-miss" appointment of the week (though that would be nice). It means that we need to see all of our actions, all of our lives, following from and toward the sacramental actions we perform in the liturgy. That is also why the same Vatican II document insists that the standard for measuring liturgical renewal should be "the full, conscious, and active participation" of all the faithful (ibid. 14). I know well as a teacher that students who actively participate in class—even if it is very active and engaged listening—are the ones who learn.

How does this connection of liturgies and life play out? One could give dozens of examples. Perhaps it means shaping how we handle a conflict at work by the model we experience in the sacrament of reconciliation. Perhaps it means remembering that our "family" name, the one whose reputation we bear in our conduct in the world, is fundamentally the identity of Christ we put on in baptism and "wear" in the world. Maybe it means knowing that our ultimate mentor, the one who truly co-missions us, is not anyone at work, but the Holy Spirit of confirmation. And it certainly means the greatest gathering for us is with our family of faith, at the feast where we are fed, dare to pray to our Father, hear our family stories retold, and share peace with all those around us.

When the sacraments become disconnected from real life, two things happen. One, they can easily become the kinds of pious actions on which the Pharisees focused. Jesus said, "The scribes and the Pharisees have taken their seat on the chair of Moses. Therefore, do and observe all things whatsoever they tell you, but do not follow their example," for "[a]ll their works are performed to be seen" and receive honor from others (Matt 23:2, 5). This desire to do visible pious actions in order to be seen by others has a chilling effect both on the Christian community itself and on its witness to the world.

But second, and more to our purposes, we fail to see the immense ecological significance packed into the sacraments. How can we reverence water so highly in the liturgical setting—and then know the local river is so toxic that we could never baptize people with its water? How can we be so careful with the eucharistic bread and wine—and then know that we throw away food carelessly and routinely while others are hungry? At its best, Catholic sacramental theology reverences the sacraments not only for their reminders of the story of our salvation, our family history, but also because they provide us with so many clues for what ecological life in the new creation should look like.

So, we've seen that Christian salvation is not about escape but renewal, and we've seen the renewal is made vividly present to us in the sacraments, as a source and model for the holy living of the rest of our lives. Once we see renewal as the goal, and genuinely sacramental living as the means, we are enabled to understand better a third piece of Christian theology: Jesus' frequent stinging criticisms of wealth and possessions. The gospel critique of wealth is a way of understanding that our trust in and valuing of worldly possessions is an "anti-salvation," a "countersacramental" system where we falsely believe in the ultimate value of material things.

Any fair reading of the gospels cannot overlook how consistently Jesus expresses concern about the dangers of material possessions and riches. These examples should not be entirely surprising, in the light of the last chapter: Jesus was a pious Jew, approached as a wise teacher of the law, and hailed as a prophet. Both the law and the prophets express clear views about the right and wrong handling of possessions. But even in this context, Jesus expresses strong views on this issue: cursing those with wealth (Luke 6:24), telling stories of the condemnation of the wealthy who fail to share their abundance (Luke 12:15-21; 16:19-31), encountering a rich young man who desires holiness but refuses to give up his "many possessions" (Luke 18:18-23), saying whoever "does not renounce all his possessions cannot be my disciple" (Luke 14:33), indicating that "it is easier for a camel to pass through the eye of a needle than for a rich person to enter the kingdom of God" (Luke 18:25). And, contrary to a common story I've heard, there is no "needle gate" at Jerusalem or any such reading that makes Jesus' words easier![9] Besides, the amazed responses of the disciples that salvation then appears impossible should lead us to view this comparison as a serious challenge, even to the norms of that age. Jesus counsels a reliance on God for daily sustenance that is meant to imitate the birds and the flowers: "I tell you, do not worry about your life and what you will eat, or about your body and what you will wear. . . . Instead, seek his kingdom, and these other things will be given you besides. . . . Sell your belongings and give alms" (Luke 12:22, 31, 33; cf. Matt 6:25-34). The New Testament also conspicuously *drops* one idea that is present in some Old Testament material: that accumulating wealth is a "sign of God's blessing."[10] Thus, as Sondra Wheeler puts it in a comprehensive study of the New Testament, wealth is seen as "peril and obligation" in the New Testament, one that is often a source of sin, but one that could be used to fulfill strict obligations of justice and generosity toward others.[11]

From the earliest days, the church has been concerned with how to read these passages. Like any biblical passages, they must be interpreted and applied. As many commentators have pointed out, there are a "multiplicity of models and mandates" for handling possessions in the New Testament.[12] Some writers stress total renunciation, others the importance of almsgiving, still others the importance of pooling possessions. But nevertheless, throughout the writings of the early church, "Christian self-definition includes unequivocal denunciation of avarice and luxury as irrational desires and displays of wealth" and especially favors the importance of almsgiving.[13] As time went on, though, and especially with the development of a so-called two-level ethic, readings often got caught between two poles. On the one hand, as most starkly shown in the case of St. Francis of Assisi, a few followed Christ's literal call for a radical poverty. On the other hand, most others were simply called to a minimal spiritual "detachment" from possessions—we can have them, but we shouldn't be too "attached" to them. One book sums up its section on the present state of actual Christian practice as having "evaded or spiritualized to death" these teachings, pretending that we can pile up "extravagant possessions," claiming such spending does not affect us in our "hearts," at the same time giving "as generously as [we] 'can'"[14]

The Catechism sorts this out more clearly than we do: "Christian life strives to order this world's goods to God and to fraternal charity" (2401). God destined the world's goods "to the whole human race," and "private property . . . does not do away with the original gift of the earth to the whole of [hu] mankind" (2402, 2403). Rather, private property is to be used so as to allow each person "to meet his basic needs and the needs of those in his charge," with the rest of his wealth to be used by "making it fruitful and communicating its benefits to others" (2402, 2404). Goods should be used "with moderation" and be shared with those in need, as an exercise of "justice" and "solidarity" (2405, 2407). In summary form, the Catechism is explaining the traditional Catholic belief that our property has a "social mortgage"—it is not simply ours to do with what we please. It is there to meet our basic needs and then to be shared for the common good. Thus, Thomas Aquinas distinguishes between what he calls "natural" and "artificial" wealth: the former is good because it meets our needs as human beings; the latter is not, because it simply creates more and more false needs that end up being infinite, thus replacing God as our highest good.[15] Instead of "artificial wealth," we should seek justice and love by using goods to meet the real human needs of others.

These sources help us put Jesus' teachings on riches in their proper perspective. The problem is twofold: one, our desire for unlimited accumulation of possessions and, two, our inability to put limits on our selfish spending so that we can give away what we don't need. Perhaps the most striking biblical model for this is Zacchaeus, a story so exciting that we are told the crowd thought the kingdom would arrive immediately! Zacchaeus is a tax collector who publicly renounces half of his possessions and promises, "If I have extorted anything from anyone I shall repay it four times over." Upon hearing this, Jesus proclaims, "Today salvation has come to this house" (Luke 19:8-9). This is *salvation*! Imagine if the wealthy today, all those who have more than they need, genuinely gave away half their wealth and also restored anything that did not meet the strict guidelines of the Catechism for honestly gained wealth (violations include "business fraud; paying unjust wages; forcing up prices . . . speculation in which one contrives to manipulate the price of goods artificially . . . ; work poorly done; tax evasion; . . . excessive expenses and waste" [2409]). All these, the Catechism says, are forms of theft "even if it does not contradict the provisions of civil law" (ibid.). Imagine if, say, bankers in charge during the 2007–2008 financial crisis stood up and did this. Imagine too how this story, in an insecure ancient context, mocks our anxiety that we simply "need" all our excess accumulation for "security." The story of Zacchaeus is a story about how salvation comes through material possessions—through fourfold restoration and massive sharing. This is a stark tale for us in a consumer society where the sky is the limit.

How are these teachings on the use of possessions connected to the environment? Hopefully we will immediately see that our present environmental crisis has everything to do with the advent of what we call a "consumer society" in which "no limits" becomes a marketing slogan, and accumulation can reach unheard-of heights. The details of this problem will be sorted out more carefully in the coming chapters. But we should keep in mind these two important claims: to moderate our own desires and to give generously—both emphasize that following Christ involves strong limits on our quest for material possessions.

Salvation is truly at stake in these matters. The salvation offered by Christianity, as we have seen, is concrete, communal, and material—as well as supernatural and spiritual. It comes in and through the material creation, not apart from it or by escaping it. It comes from recognizing the way sin distorts our view of the importance of wealth and possessions, pushing us to another, alternative way of "storing up treasure in heaven," especially through the "sacrament" of the poor and needy.[16] In all of this, the Old Testament story of the good created order and God's covenant to restore it through the law is brought to fulfillment and completion. It is not a different story, and certainly not a contrary story. The Bible invites us into a single story of God's creation and salvation, one that should establish the patterns for all of our lives, including our environmental use and care. In Part 2, we move to exploring the practical implications for our present patterns of life.

Transition

What, Then, Shall We Do?

Go to your local bookstore or find a website devoted to helping the planet. You'll quickly discover that contemporary environmentalism loves lists of "things you can do" and, of course, a lot of "thou shalt nots," things you should stop doing or do less of. These can be very long lists! Famously, the closing credits of the 2006 global warming film *An Inconvenient Truth* featured a rolling list of dozens of "things you can do to make a difference," from insulating your house to taking reusable bags to the store. In his book *How Bad Are Bananas?* Mike Berners-Lee compiles an extraordinary recipe book of the carbon footprint of nearly everything we do, from sending a text message to flying to Europe to having a major operation.[1] Bananas turn out to be not bad at all, because they grow so easily and they last, enabling low-carbon transport by ship. Not so much those asparagus spears or berries air-shipped in—recall that speed is a disease! Still, my two-mile walk (instead of driving) to the coffee shop today to write this chapter saved an even larger amount of carbon emissions than a pint of those air-shipped berries. In another example of to-do lists, Lori Bongiorno spends 150 pages outlining "green, greener, and greenest" practices for every aspect of your household, from personal care products to baby care to even pest control.[2]

I joke that, in the past, it used to be the Catholic priest in the confessional who had thousands of minute sins listed in his manual; but today, it is the environmentalist! The impulse toward action in environmentalism is a good thing. While reading the earlier chapters of this book, I hope you sensed the need for action. Christian life also calls for action. Think of the crowds in Jerusalem who first heard Peter proclaim the resurrection. We are told they were "cut to the heart" and responded, "What are we to *do?*" (Acts 2:37). Following the risen Christ is not about receiving information; it's about being sent on a mission. Action is essential to the Christian life. Jesus closes his Sermon on the Mount by contrasting those who just listen to his words with those who listen *and act* (Matt 7:24-27). Catholicism is not just a set of beliefs we hold in our heads. It is, as the early church described it, "the *way.*"

At the same time, I know these eco-lists annoy people. They seem daunting in their exhaustiveness. It always seems like we are running into compromises, and constant guilt. Moreover, what's really important and what's not? Does my hamburger really matter? My lightbulbs? My car? Aren't all these problems much, much bigger than that? Besides, what does it matter if I buy an efficient car when my neighbor down the street just got a huge SUV? And isn't all this hairsplitting a bit like the Pharisees in the gospels—all righteous display, but not concentrating on what "really matters" to Jesus, which is loving others?

The following chapters are a hopeful attempt to identify action that really does matter. Indeed, presuming that most readers of this book are relatively well-off North Americans or Europeans, your actions are easily the most important in the world, given that the responsibility for overuse of God's earth is wildly skewed toward our societies. Our environmental actions may matter more than anyone else on the planet because, as James Garvey puts it, we "have much more economic power than the vast majority of people on the planet."[3] If we lived our lives differently, the largest political roadblock to international cooperation on this issue would also be removed. Pope Benedict insists on the need for a "sustainable comprehensive management of the environment" that requires "better internationally coordinated management of the earth's resources."[4] Many environmental problems are global and so require global solutions; however, these are blocked when those in wealthy countries selfishly cling to their rights to continue to degrade the environment.

What these chapters *don't* do, however, is give an exact to-do list. I'm doing something different here for three reasons. First, the most important environmental choices we make aren't about individual things; rather, they are about persistent *patterns* of choices, patterns we weave into our lives. Remember that priest with his list of sins for the confessional? One of the persistent criticisms of that approach to Catholic morality was that it was too "act-centered," that is, it focused on isolated, individual actions. Moral theology since Vatican II has become much more focused on the *person* and one's overall moral development (which of course includes actions), as well as recovering the ancient tradition of the importance of *virtues*, the habits that make up our basic moral character. So too, when practicing care for creation, we need to identify and root out the sinful, disordered patterns in our own lives, the environmental vices, and vigorously break out of them into alternative patterns. What is needed from all of us is holiness; holiness (unless it is like the Pharisees!) is not a checklist of tasks but more like a creative line of work or an activity in which we are *passionately* involved. It's something that we throw our whole selves into, and changes each of us as a person. We might also think of this like dating a new person or even learning a new language or culture. There are actions we take, of course, but there's not a to-do list. Instead, there is a new way of living in the world. We need not think of this as completely abandoning our "old self." But there is real adjustment and change needed, and we can best identify these changes if we understand the dominant *patterns* of our ecological lives.

Second, I'm focusing on patterns because it helps us avoid possible despair when we see that nearly all the important environmental issues we face involve large, often global, structures. These can make us feel powerless. Pope John Paul II called them "structures of sin," in that they give "the impression of creating, in persons and institutions, an obstacle which is difficult to overcome" in seeking the common good (*Sollicitudo Rei Socialis* 36). Recall that Polish communism was such a structure. But the pope insisted that people were not powerless. He rightly said that these mechanisms "are rooted in personal sin and thus always linked to the concrete acts of individuals who introduce these structures, consolidate them and make them difficult to remove" (ibid., 36). In using the theological language of sin, the pope insists that analyzing social problems cannot just remain at the surface of mechanics, but requires "a more profound analysis" and "conversion" (ibid., 36, 38). It is the responsibility of Catholics to resist these structures. If we are able to name and resist structures of sin, God will help us do the impossible. But to change them, we must be able to see the alternate *patterns* of life that we need to embrace, in the place right where we are. The patterns I identify in these chapters are kind of like levers for moving structures—that is, they are like tools which, if placed rightly, enable us to move things that seem far too heavy to move.

Third, attention to patterns also acknowledges that there is no one-size-fits-all, silver-bullet answer to the question, "What should we do?" It is a striking feature of our culture that we want these kinds of single explanation solutions. What is the key to losing weight? We go through endless diet fads, each one giving a "new" answer. What we probably all know is that a varied but restrained diet, combined with regular physical activity, is pretty much the answer for most people. Eliminating this or that single "root of all evil" food or ingredient doesn't fix everything. Moreover, we have different bodies to begin with, and we all think about how we should eat after already acquiring a set of eating habits, some good, some not so good. I have no problem with calories but have inherited my father's elevated cholesterol. I eat hardly any red meat, but I do love dairy and butter-rich baked goods. It became obvious what patterns I needed to look at to pull my cholesterol down. Out with the muffins and cheese, in with the oats and almonds.

Acting on core Christian environmental beliefs is like this. We all start in different places, and (like one's health, with obesity and cholesterol) there isn't one "environmental problem" but rather a *set* of interrelated but distinct problems. Some people drive huge vehicles, but hardly ever fly; some people bike everywhere, but take frequent global flights. Some people love to cook, but won't pick food that is local or in season; other people simply can't cook and end up with fast food or disposable frozen dinners. Some people may lovingly tend a few acres and protect their own local countryside, but then take the train to the city to trade stocks or make loans for vastly destructive industrial food enterprises. Even these examples start sounding too much like a list—but they involve different patterns of life that need attention if we are going to effect change. Asking the banker to replace his lightbulbs or take reusable grocery bags to the store isn't really where one should start; she should start with banking and investment for environmental sustainability. Hopefully, this approach inspires a good bit of humility in us, too, since we may overestimate our neighbor's environmental shortcomings while underestimating our own!

I identify four key patterns in the following chapters that intersect with many of the major environmental problems of our time. However, I should mention that not every problem receives attention here, given the modest scope of this text. Many other environmental books begin with a lengthy chapter listing the many, overlapping problems that creation faces.[5]

Two issues that I do not treat in much detail deserve at least a mention. One is the extinction of species and loss of what is usually called "biodiversity." Science writers have termed this era the "sixth great extinction." Past extinctions happened because of massive events like meteor strikes or glacial ice ages; today, the "catastrophe" is the outsized activity of humans. At present, an average of three species per day go extinct, a rate at least one hundred to one thousand times greater than the natural rate of species extinction. This "biotic holocaust" affects the plant kingdom as well, as a small number of types of apples, tomatoes, and the like are cultivated, leading to the loss of thousands of other variants that evolved over time in different places.[6] The loss of biodiversity is not simply a kind of insult to the bountiful design of the Creator, ignoring the beauty and complexity of the natural order, but is also a long-term threat to entire ecosystems, which often depend on diversity to survive droughts, pests, and diseases.

Another issue with potentially grave consequences is the problem of water. Theologian Christiana Peppard notes that fresh water is a scarce resource, constituting only 2.5 percent of the world's total water, and yet we are now using it in unsustainable ways, drawing especially on depleting underground aquifers and dammed river reservoirs. Only a small percentage of our total use is what she calls "renewable water," that is, the water we can count on through rainfall, evaporation, and ice runoff.[7] Like the carbon and nitrogen cycles we will explore, the water cycle is also running way too fast—and obviously a scarcity of water is a huge problem for human life! While I do not deal directly with these problems of species extinction and hydrologic cycles, many of the problematic patterns I identify in these chapters are also the patterns that create problems for water and for species diversity. For example, Peppard names the increase in use of water as "the meat and microchips problem,"[8] since we often do not see that our most *intensive* water demands are not from leaving the faucet on, but from the huge amounts of water necessary to raise livestock and manufacture computer components (which must be engineered and cleaned to an incredible level of precision).

So, *what, then, shall we do*? Give up our computers? Or just our smartphones and the dozens of other "toys" that now have microchips in them? As I noted, there are in fact thousands of things we can do to "be green." But in these chapters, I want to invite us all into a few crucial patterns of our lives that lie at the heart of the matter. Perhaps confirming the biblical images we read earlier, these patterns also tend to lie at the heart of our daily lives, too—and their centrality is why "it's not easy being green." But like so many other aspects of Christian discipleship, the difficulty is meant to liberate us into a much greater joy.

Part
Two

chapter 5

Food and Fuel

*[I]t becomes clear that short-term economic gains
must be placed within the context of better long-
term planning for food security with regard to both
quantity and quality. The order of creation demands
that priority be given to those human activities
that do not cause irreversible damage to nature, but
which are instead woven into the social, cultural,
and religious fabric of the different communities.
In this way, a sober balance is achieved between
consumption and the sustainability of resources.*

—Benedict XVI[1]

What do human beings need in creation to survive? We could
start with air. In recent decades, there seems to be an obvious
success that makes people think "we can solve environmental
problems": the fight against localized air pollution. While the
problem is far from solved, citizens in most US cities breathe
cleaner air than most have in cities over the past two hundred
years. But there has also been other progress. Air is not only
visibly cleaner but also has been purified of certain poisons.
Changes in car emission systems have been required, lead has
been taken out of gasoline, and states run regular exhaust test-
ing for vehicles. Thankfully, a few decades ago, people seemed
to have less skepticism about these measures!

Now, even this "success" is complicated. Cities may be cleaner, but a lot of polluting industry still goes on—we've just relocated it to other countries! One look at major Chinese industrial centers will give us at least some pause in believing that air quality is solved. There, many cities are constantly enshrouded in a devastating industrial smog: "Chinese cities have some of the world's most polluted air. The haze is often so thick it blots out the sun. On especially bad days in cities such as Harbin, in northeast China, residents can't even see across the street. Airports struggle regularly to land planes in thick fog."[2] One recent report identifies a city where air pollution is *forty times* the safe limit established by the World Health Organization![3] To "solve" the problem, sometimes crazy and always expensive proposals abound, from giant vacuum cleaners to leveling mountains around polluted cities stuck in valleys. How ironic a way to "solve" an environmental problem! Still, the basic pattern of humans breathing clean air has been accepted and has spurred much environmental improvement in developed countries.

In this chapter, I want to start our tour of patterns with another thing humans need from their physical environment: *calories*. A calorie is a unit of energy. Human life is a quest to make sure we have enough calories; too few calories may not mean death, but it will almost certainly mean a lot more misery. Humans need this energy, and we don't produce it internally. We need it first and foremost from our food but, indirectly, we also need energy from fire. Fire produces calories, which heats our food, but also heats us, a necessity over much of the earth's surface. The mastery of fire's energy further allows us to do something else: make tools far more sophisticated than what we can hew from stone. These tools then make our provision of food calories from hunting and farming more effective. (In a larger sense, all these calories come from fire—they come from the sun!)

Given these necessities, it makes a lot of sense to start by looking at our patterns in relation to food and fuel. Recall that I began the book by encouraging a leisurely, attentive stroll to encounter the beauty and variety of nature. Presumably you had enough to eat in order to appreciate it! Let's think about this question: Where did that food come from? If you yourself raised it, you probably didn't need the stroll to learn lessons about nature! But if you are like most of us, your food came from a cabinet or a fridge, and before that from a large storage shed we call a supermarket. It got there from wherever it originated (probably far away) on a very large vehicle, or many such vehicles, nearly all of which are fueled by a special source of calories that we call "fossil fuel." More than likely, a smaller version of such a vehicle got you and your food home from the market. Where did *that* rich source of calories come from? This fossil fuel energy is not only in your car, it's in your stove, your fridge, your cabinets (unless you are really resourceful with saws and your backyard trees). Not only do these use fossil fuels but so does the transportation that makes it possible to have and use so much that we did not make ourselves—there are lots and lots of calories behind all that.

Let's appreciate how unusual this pattern is in the sweep of human history. For most of that time, food and fuel sources almost *had* to be local, apart from what could be transported by water. (It is not surprising that the Roman Empire basically surrounded the Mediterranean Sea!) Many people basically fed themselves; any other goods they might have made themselves, or at least they knew who made them. Let us not romanticize this picture. Usually, to support the leisure of the (very few) rich, most people had to endure hard labor in their fields to make any kind of surplus. Crop failures in one place would mean devastating famine, as in the story of Joseph and his brothers in Genesis. Most people in a society needed to spend most of their time simply raising food. In the eighteenth century, it was conventionally thought that 75 to 80 percent of a society's labor force would be devoted to farming. Even in 1910 in the United States, after trains and the expansion over some of the richest farmland in the world, it still took around a third of the country's workforce to feed ourselves.[4] Compare this to today: farmers account for less than 1 percent of the population![5] The move to massive factory farms has freed a large portion of the population to spend time doing other things. (For example, watching TV, which occupies three and a half hours of every day for the average American.[6] If the average American spent just one hour a day tending a backyard garden and preserving its food, many of the problems cited in this chapter would be solved. But I digress.)

The modern miracles of our food and fossil fuel systems should not be underestimated. But neither should their environmental impact. Consider the impact of burning fossil fuels. In the past, almost everyone's "carbon footprint" was the size of a person today living in the least developed countries—around 40 *times* less than our current average in the United States. Not 40 percent less, 40 *times* less—one American burns through what forty people do in poor countries. It means the 300 million Americans burn through as much fossil fuel as 12 billion poor, except there are only 7 billion people *total* on the planet!

We also consume vast amounts of food calories, to some extent because food marketers figure out a way to sell them to us. Our per capita calorie intake has risen 10 percent since the 1970s, right along with obesity figures. A well-known map put together by the Centers for Disease Control graphically represents the growth in obesity from 1990 to 2010. In 1990, *every* single state had an obesity rate of under 20 percent, and the majority were under 15 percent. The states gradually changed color over time, and by 2010, the last state (Colorado) finally went over 20 percent, with a near-majority of states creeping past 30 percent.[7] These are not measures of people who have put on a few extra pounds; this is a measure of genuine obesity. Many researchers point out that this is not simply a loss of self-control but an eagerness on the part of food manufacturers to convert more and more mass-produced calories into dollars. Moreover, estimates suggest we waste at least a quarter of the food calories we produce, and even with that waste, we still generate a food surplus that can be exported cheaply to poor countries, feeding the world but undermining their local farms.

What is the morality involved in all this? Isn't a lot of this good, a result of efficiency, of more productive processes? Aren't we always discovering new technologies to tap further fossil fuel sources, as is now happening with shale oil and gas in parts of the United States? And isn't it good that we have liberated so many people from the toil of food production and walking? Tools for increased productivity and mobility can be good. For sure, my life relies on these things too. So why is there an issue?

Let's call to mind our earlier insights into the spiritual diseases of scale, speed, and selfish individualism—these helped us see that our distorted participation in creation was a matter of surpassing limits. Our really critical environmental problems do not involve straight-out "bad" actions, but rather doing too much of things that are ordinary human goods. They are scale and speed problems, as we pointed out earlier. Bill McKibben famously analyzed our entire economic system by saying that we are like someone who has had two drinks, feels great, and so decides that ten drinks will make him feel five times better.[8] Our food and fuel systems follow the drunk's mistaken logic. But what limits are we surpassing with our patterns of food and fuel use, and why can't we see these limits clearly? In order to answer this question, we will look closely at the natural patterns of the soil and the atmosphere and then turn to the problem of "proxies"—people don't directly choose to exhaust the earth; they let others do so on their behalf. It is not difficult to get people to respond to environmental problems in their backyards; it is far more difficult to manage problems that we can't (or won't) see.

Because our food and fuel systems involve problems with large natural patterns and "proxies" who consume on our behalf, they differ a lot from easier-to-recognize environmental problems. Let us consider obviously deadly environmental harms. If someone was putting deadly chemicals (I mean, immediately deadly) into our food or into the air, we'd probably end up doing something to stop it. The implementation of pure food and drug laws was one of the first big successes of the twentieth century.

One of the landmarks of the contemporary environmental movement was Rachel Carson's 1962 *Silent Spring,* which exposed the deadly effects of pesticides like DDT on wildlife, with potential implications for humans as well. Dead birds and poisoned children have a way of focusing our attention!

But the key environmental problem with our food and fuel systems turns out to center on putting carbon dioxide into the air (which not only doesn't kill us but is essential for plant life) and putting nitrogen into the soil (which, far from a poison, is the essential nutrient for plants and is captured by us from the air, where it makes up nearly four-fifths of the air and just sits there inert). How can this be a problem?

It is here where an appreciation of the intricate beauty of creation, beyond the "pow" feeling, is needed to sense the problem. Take the nitrogen cycle. Soil fertility depends on a nitrogen cycle, where nitrogen drawn out of the soil by growing plants is then replenished. Plants need a number of nutrients, but "none is as important as nitrogen because of its role in building proteins and regulating growth and metabolism in plants."[9] Soils can maintain their fertility virtually indefinitely, if they are planted with certain sorts of crops that replenish (rather than use up) nitrogen, as well as if rich-in-nitrogen manure and compost waste is spread on them. Humans mastered this cycle over the course of many centuries. Rightly tended, this abundance doesn't cease; it can even be enhanced. The soil is the ultimate in a renewable resource (next to the sun, of course). To till the soil in this sustainable way is to appreciate the beauty of creation and its "grammar," as Pope Benedict put it. It is to work with the natural order to sustain fertility and life. Soil fertility is the ultimate renewable resource, potentially feeding humans indefinitely simply from the combination of sun and skilled labor (and some animal manure).

Here, however, there is a limit. There's a limit to how much a field can yield before it must be rested. There's an overall limit to how much nitrogen is "fixed" in nature. It must be tended carefully to achieve this renewability, or else its fertility is quickly "used up" (as in the plowing of the fragile American prairie soil, which became dust in the course of only a generation or two). The limits of this nitrogen cycle also seemed to be a limit on how much total food humans can produce—and thus, at least to some thinkers of the nineteenth century, an impending tragedy for humanity, since as populations prospered, they grew, and as they grew, the land would run low, and there would be starvation. It also meant that much cultural time was spent retaining sources of nutrients and managing this nitrogen cycle. In premodern land-poor Asian nations like Korea and Japan, composting waste from villages back to fields was practiced with "a most religious fidelity."[10]

The breaking of the strong triple bond of atmospheric nitrogen—and thus of the soil nitrogen cycle—came only in 1913. German chemists learned how to capture (under high heat and pressure) nitrogen out of the air and put it in bags, which could be spread on fields to "fertilize" them. This seemed at first simply a way to "fix up" more marginal farmlands and keep them in production, but the seduction of significant yield increases, less uncertainty, and freedom from complicated systems of farm and crop management (i.e., with fertilizers, hundreds of acres of corn could just be planted over and over, every year) meant that by the post–World War II era, 95 percent of American soils were subject to fertilizer use.[11] The rate of increase in the developing world has been even faster.

This use has created an unprecedented increase in overall food production, supporting a global population that now adds a billion people every thirteen to fifteen years. The ill effects, however, are many. First and foremost, the fertilizers destroy soil biodiversity, leaving soils less able to absorb water and oxygen. From this, soil microbes decrease, making it more difficult for soils to hold together, eventually leading to topsoil erosion. Once topsoil erodes, nutrients are no longer available to plants. Thus, fertilizers undermine natural soil biodiversity and acidify soils, problems that are "remedied" by more and more complex fertilizers.[12]

Further, a considerable amount of fertilizer never actually is taken up by the plant. The excess runs off, accumulating in water supplies as dangerous nitrates; evaporating as nitrous oxide, a very powerful greenhouse gas (more on that later); or, perhaps most devastatingly, accumulating in the major estuaries and river deltas, like the Mississippi River delta and the Chesapeake Bay, where it more or less "kills" everything in the water by depriving it of oxygen and encouraging algae growth.[13] The "dead zone" at the mouth of the Mississippi is now larger than the state of New Jersey.

Nitrogen fertilizers can be seen as a great human invention, insofar as they have made possible a food production system of astonishing abundance for an exploding population. But the current existence of nearly double the natural amount of "active" nitrogen has long-term ill effects. We can sum this up by saying, *while its immediate effects seem attractive, the process as a whole is unsustainable.* Scientists report in the journal *Nature* that, of nine major environmental systems, the "overshoot" of the nitrogen cycle beyond a "safe planetary boundary" is the second worst problem, exceeding even climate change.[14] Ultimately, the present quantity of fertilizer use is simply incompatible with lake, river, and ocean health, endangering not only the systems that depend on marine life but also the enormous gift of the protein supply to humans from the world's fisheries.

A similar, but much more well-known, story of a path to unsustainable excess can be told about the natural carbon cycle. The planet as a whole "breathes," because plants and animal life give each other the carbon dioxide and oxygen each, respectively, needs. Like the nitrogen cycle, the elegant interdependence of natural systems is displayed, as waste products from some parts of creation nourish the life of other parts. The carbon cycle is also important because the effect of the relatively small amount of carbon dioxide in the atmospheric mix traps *just enough* of the sun's rays to give our planet its distinctive and essential temperature range. Without this layer, Earth's day-night temperature difference would fluctuate much more dramatically, since the atmosphere traps and saves some of the day's heat from the sun. Mars lacks this greenhouse, and so daytime temperatures frequently drop more than 100 degrees Celsius at night!

For the entire period of human civilization, carbon dioxide has made up 260–280 parts per million (ppm) of the atmosphere. (Concentration of any gas in air is typically expressed as "parts" of the gas "per million.") However, the level started increasing very gradually but steadily in the late 1700s, reaching 300 ppm around 1910.[15] The rate of increase really began to take off, however, after World War II; after 1960, the gains amounted to 10–15 ppm *per decade*; in the 2000s, it increased 21 ppm in just a single decade. As Michael Northcott points out, we've put five *times* more carbon into the atmosphere in the last forty years as we did in the preceding two hundred. All signs are that the main "carbon sinks"—not only forests but also the oceans, both of which have done "work" to suck carbon out of the air—are becoming less able to take up this extra carbon, and so it remains in the atmosphere. In other words, nature gives us some margin of error, where we might put a bit of extra carbon into the air, but still maintain a balance. However, that margin seems used up. The level topped 400 ppm in 2013, a level never remotely approached at any point in humanity's history. The last time carbon concentrations were this high was around fourteen million years ago, at which time there were no ice caps, seas were seventy feet higher, and temperatures were 3–6 degrees Celsius higher.[16]

Why does carbon dioxide matter? The chief effect is to thicken the atmosphere and trap more heat—hence, the name "the greenhouse effect." At this point, global temperatures have risen 0.8 degrees Celsius overall, with much of this rise in the past three decades. While attempts to model a system as complex as this are challenging, nearly all reputable climate scientists suggest that temperatures will rise 2–4 degrees by 2100, even given successful efforts to stabilize emissions at their present levels. Without such efforts, "business as usual" could bring a 3–6 degree rise, and potentially even more dramatic rises of 6–11 degrees if certain "tipping points" are passed, such as the thawing of Arctic permafrost (releasing huge amounts of carbon and methane) or larger-than-expected ice melts. That's just by 2100. Even on the stable scenario, the temperature rise is 6 degrees (over 10 degrees Fahrenheit) by 2200.[17]

There is little doubt that the primary force behind such unprecedented and (in geologic terms) rapid change is the large-scale burning of fossil fuels. As with the nitrogen cycle, the key "break" in the self-maintaining carbon cycle is the introduction of huge amounts of "extra" material—in this case, material drawn from below the earth's surface. And like nitrogen fertilizers, there is no doubt that the introduction of fossil fuels has made possible an unprecedented level of development and world population (not least because they are needed to create the energy to make the fertilizers, as well as to manage the planting and harvesting and distribution of huge amounts of crops!). And like nitrogen, the major problem here is with the waste "sink" when the cycle runs too fast—that is, when humans "breathe out" carbon dioxide faster than plants and the oceans can breathe it in.

However, climate change and the carbon cycle attract more attention simply because the potential ramifications of the over-use of carbon are so large and potentially dramatic. Warming may seem a mere inconvenience, or even a benefit. Top climate economist William Nordhaus acknowledges that, in the short term, "managed systems" like agriculture may overall see a short-term benefit from a small amount of warming. However, the chief problems occur with what Nordhaus calls "unmanageable systems"—sea level rise, ocean acidification, increasingly unpredictable and severe weather patterns, shifts in local ecosystems (i.e., the loss of mountain runoff in dry areas, the spread of insects to newly warm areas where plants have no defenses against them), and species extinction.[18] All of these problems, moreover, have disproportionate effects on poorer nations, particularly in the global South. There, events like Hurricane Sandy, which struck New York and New Jersey in 2012, cannot be met with the immense resources of a wealthy nation. On top of this, the very warming itself is likely to have the most dire effect on places that already suffer from intense heat.

Fossil fuels have another unique aspect, too: unlike the soil and plant resources, they are not renewable. They were formed over many eons; once they are burned, they do not regrow. Over the past century, humans have drawn down much of what is easily accessible, and therefore new energy finds are increasingly expensive and produce less EROEI, that is, "energy return on energy invested" to extract the resources. In 1930, the EROEI for oil was 100 to 1—getting 100 times as much energy as is put into the process of recovering the oil. Today, because deposits are more remote and harder to extract, it is down to 15 to 1.[19] Despite recent new discoveries that have unexpectedly increased US domestic production of oil, the price has not fallen, as supply and demand would lead us to expect. Why? Because this new oil is only "economic" to extract above a certain price—the extraction itself is expensive.[20] Given the extraordinary and unique benefits of fossil fuel use, one could easily imagine nations deciding that these reserves should be conserved. If they were, they would last virtually indefinitely for basic human needs. Sadly, however, we seem pleased to extract and use this gift as quickly as possible, for whatever we might want, in the (plainly false) belief that more will always be available.

Attempts to address both of these problems have been resisted, and we should easily see why. It is not that people do not see the problem; it's painful to confront because the problem is so enmeshed in our daily lives—in our eating, our housing, our transportation. We would have to acknowledge that our "way of life" is largely unsustainable and needs changing. As Wendell Berry writes, "The dominant response, in short, is a dogged belief that what we call 'the American way of life' will prove somehow indestructible. We will keep on consuming, spending, wasting, and driving, as before, at any cost to anything and everybody but ourselves."[21] Moreover, it is pretty clear that we can go on doing this for some time, and everything can "seem" to be manageable. It is very hard for humans to think about their actions having effects in 2200. And yet 2200 is not really that far off, especially in "Catholic time." Hence, the popular analogy with smoking, a habit that can be indulged for some time with seemingly little ill effect but that is often quietly deadly in the long run.

Addressing these problems is also hard because few of us use fertilizer, mine coal, or even see the oil and natural gas that burn in our homes and cars. As is the case with factory farming, if most of us were regularly confronted with the destructive character of certain processes in our lives—much less their long-term effects—we might be far more concerned about our reliance on them. But instead we allow others to be concerned about that on our behalf. Others grow the food and mine the coal, just as others raise and slaughter the animals.

Hence, we need to think about a second problem: what Wendell Berry calls our "proxies"—what we would not do ourselves, but what we readily allow others to do on our behalf. Berry terms our present system an "absentee economy," noting correctly that "most people aren't using or destroying what they can see."[22] The problem is that "we have allowed our suppliers to enlarge our economic boundaries so far that we cannot be responsible for our effects on the world."[23] Consequently, "most of us know vaguely, if at all, where [the things we buy] come from; and most of us know not at all what damage is involved in their production. We are almost entirely dependent on an economy of which we are almost entirely ignorant." He insists that such a situation requires us to ask the question, "What proxies have we issued, and to whom, to use the earth on our behalf?"[24]

The question of our environmental proxies opens up two concerns for Catholics. One links back to an earlier issue: care for creation is fundamentally grounded in seeing rightly. Since, as we noted earlier, few people openly seek to destroy the creation, its destruction must go on "behind closed doors," as it were. It is difficult to develop the proper spiritual affection for the environment if we "manage" it invisibly. Hence, one important step is simply to expose these patterns, so that people can see what is actually required for our caloric burn. We need to look at dead zones in oceans, mountaintop removal, dense smog in China—and realize these are the effects of others providing us with elements of our lifestyle.

The second concern involves the question of who is responsible. Morality exists because we are responsible (accountable) for our actions. Needing food and fuel is not morally problematic, of course. But we view certain ways of obtaining it as morally wrong (i.e., stealing). More directly, we view certain ways of abusing common resources as destructive and wrong (e.g., littering in a park). The riches of the earth, on which we are reliant, are gifts from God to all, as we have seen. And it follows that we have responsibilities to care for and not abuse those resources. We do recognize these responsibilities in relation to our immediate surroundings—what we can see. However, we fail to honor those same responsibilities in relation to what we cannot see.

Are we really responsible for these problems? Catholic moral theology has long pondered this question of how to assess responsibility. At the simplest level, let's consider the morality of buying stolen goods. Most of us, happily, would not buy a computer from John, if we knew Jane and we knew Jane had had her computer stolen and we realized John was selling Jane's computer. You didn't see John take the computer. John might say to you, "Oh, I just found this thing sitting out in a trash heap." But you would say, "Um, OK, but this computer belongs to Jane." You feel certain that Jane did not just put it in the garbage. Presumably, you would not buy goods stolen from your friend.

In many cases, of course, one may have considerably less *knowledge* than in this imaginary case. Catholic theology distinguishes between vincible and invincible ignorance. Vincible ignorance refers to things you might not know, but that you have a responsibility to know and can come to know. Invincible ignorance, on the other hand, refers to what you could not possibly have known.

Presuming you know or have a reasonable suspicion that something has been brought to you via moral wrong, is it ever acceptable to cooperate anyway? Here, traditional moral theology draws on a further, more complex set of distinctions about cooperation. Consider a man who hops in a cab at a fancy hotel and says, "Take me to some prostitutes." Should the cabdriver comply? The first distinction is between formal and material cooperation. The people running the prostitution ring may themselves not engage in prostitution, but they *formally* cooperate in the bad action—that is, the very act of running the prostitution ring indicates an *intention* that people should engage in prostitution. They must intend the prostitution in order to do what they do. Formal cooperation with evil is never acceptable in the Catholic tradition. But there is no such *intention* on the part of the cabdriver; his cooperation is merely *material*. A related distinction is that between proximate and remote cooperation, which refers more "mechanically" to one's place in the chain of events that lead to bad action.

However, even material and remote cooperation can be morally problematic if it does not satisfy two further points: (1) the cooperating act itself must be good, and (2) there must be a proportionate reason for cooperating. The cabdriver feeds his family on his fares, which is a good effect, one that might not apply if, for example, a friend asked you to help him seek out some paid sex. However, if there is a line of cabs waiting at the hotel entrance, and the cabbie is assured of getting fares, he might still say, "Can't take you there, buddy. I don't do that." If the man then pulls out a gun and says, "Take me there or I'll kill you," suddenly the proportionality changes! (Or if the cabdriver is under some kind of legal obligation to take fares, with the threat that his license will be revoked otherwise, the proportionality is also different.)

The questions of responsibility raised in a situation of reliance on food and energy proxies are like these. To take a more obvious example, the actions of factory farms and slaughterhouses are clearly in violation of the Catechism's basic statement about the treatment of animals, to whom we "owe kindness" and whose "integrity" requires that they not "suffer or die need-lessly" (2415–18). It is acceptable to use animals for human purposes, even to eat them, but there is a responsibility to treat them with decency. In addition, many people signal their belief that animals should be treated humanely in their care for pets and their outright rejection of cruelty to pets. There is no theo-logical reason to hold that a domestic cat, for example, has more worth and dignity than a cow or a pig. If cruelty to one is rejected, then all animal cruelty should be rejected.

The question then becomes, should one consume factory-farmed animals? The first question of ignorance is, in most cases, similar to the stolen computer case: while one likely does not see it, one can be fairly assured that most meat commonly consumed today is produced under conditions that do not conform to a notion of animal dignity. The label "natural" or even "humane" is no assurance, although other claims (like "organic" or simply a high price) offer better possibilities of protection. As with many items in our marketplace, we look either to brands or to local knowledge. While I have not visited Bell & Evans chicken farms personally, I do know what the company states about the importantly different methods it uses to raise its chickens, and I do know people are out there paying some attention to these claims. Is this "assurance"? No, but the extra interest, effort, and cost certainly indicate that I am trying to exercise responsibility for my proxy over how others raise the chickens I eat.

The language of proportionality means that moral responsi-bility is not simply "yes" or "no." Consider other circumstances: What is my responsibility if someone else is serving me the chicken, and I don't know where it comes from? Is there a real need for the nutritional value of the unknown chicken (given that Americans eat too much meat)? But what about my re-sponsibility to receive graciously the hospitality of the host? Is there a difference between eating the unknown chicken at your grandmother's house versus eating it at a food service function at your workplace? The point of the language of cooperation is not finding ways to wriggle out of responsibility through technicalities; rather, it is an attempt to take seriously our real if incomplete responsibilities for our "proxies."

The questions raised by the distortions of the nitrogen and carbon cycles involved in much food and fuel usage are even more complicated, though the same principles about cooperation apply. Discussion can often lead quickly into "purity" battles, where it can sometimes seem that eating and using fossil fuels are evil in themselves (they're not!), or where the better becomes the enemy of the perfect.

How might we consider them in a balanced way? Compared with the issue of animal cruelty in factories, this issue does not involve a straightforward evil. The prudent use of fertilizers and fossil fuels is reasonable. But this cannot mean we have no responsibility for these natural cycles. Current practices are clearly imprudent! The first step here is to acknowledge real responsibility for these problems. To deny responsibility is akin to saying that there is nothing wrong with current practices, or that there is "nothing we can do" about them. Benedict XVI states clearly, "The natural environment is given by God to everyone, and our use of it entails a *personal responsibility* toward humanity as a whole, and in particular toward the poor and toward future generations."[25] The responsibility toward future generations should be particularly sobering on the issue of global warming. Because the problem develops slowly but surely, the real widespread dangers appear several generations into the future. Catholic theology maintains our responsibility for considering these generations in our current actions.

The second step is to recognize that these distortions are rooted in excessive use, and that our responsibility is to restrain ourselves, using what is truly necessary and questioning frivolity and waste. Pope Francis has derided the "culture of waste," noting it "has made us insensitive to wasting and throwing out foodstuffs, which is especially condemnable when, in every part of the world, unfortunately, many people and families suffer [from] hunger and malnutrition. There was a time when our grandparents were very careful not to throw away any leftover food. Consumerism has induced us to be accustomed to excess and to the daily waste of food, whose value, which goes far beyond mere financial parameters, we are no longer able to judge correctly. Let us remember well, however, that whenever food is thrown out it is as if it were stolen from the table of the poor, from the hungry!"[26] This is no trivial matter: as noted earlier, many estimates suggest a quarter or more of the food we produce with excess fertilization and other unsustainable methods is wasted. Some of the rest of it goes into so-called "junk food"—food that is useless for us nutritionally—and into excess food that causes obesity. Almost everyone can begin examining their choices and taking steps immediately to reduce usage.

Pope Benedict, in his encyclical *Caritas in Veritate*, bluntly stated that, in terms of carbon emissions, "the technologically advanced nations can and must lower their domestic energy consumption" (49). The obvious places to begin are with transportation and home energy use: the Union of Concerned Scientists estimates that 60 percent of an American's energy use is for these two things. We will look at our dwelling patterns closely in the next chapter. But suffice it to say: smaller houses, smaller cars, less driving. It also would make a difference if people stopped buying so many consumer items that are of so little use or are disposable. John Paul II noted that "the ecological question which accompanies the problem of consumerism" is "closely connected" to it, since "man consumes the resources of the earth and his own life in an excessive and disordered way" (*Centesimus Annus* 37). The pope requires us to distinguish "new and higher forms of satisfying human needs from artificial new needs which hinder the formation of a mature personality" (ibid., 36). This is a modern way of talking about Jesus' warnings about the dangers of material possessions for the Christian walk.

Using less need not be seen simply as a sacrifice, but as an opportunity. In a statement about the energy crisis, the US bishops write, "If preservation of the common good, both domestic and global, requires that we as individuals make sacrifices related to energy use, we should do so cheerfully. . . . Insofar as these adjustments affect excess possessions, we should welcome them. They are a blessing."[27] Research overwhelmingly supports the idea that we are much happier when our lives are less "cluttered" with unnecessary objects and concerns about "keeping up with the Joneses." Materialism of this sort is almost like an addiction, especially in that once we begin to pursue this path to happiness, we constantly need to repeat and speed it up in order to keep feeling happy. Psychologist Tim Kasser has demonstrated in detailed studies that people with more "materialistic values" end up scoring worse on measures of overall satisfaction and happiness.[28]

On the other hand, changing to more sustainable food consumption can also create happiness. Learning to cook with the seasons, cutting back on meats, getting to know local farmers at the farmers' market or food co-op—all these things can make food something God intended it to be, a means of communion, rather than merely "filling our tanks" out of boxes from the supermarket. Such a bounty can also be shared. Fred Bahnson tells the inspiring story of the Welcome Table at St. James Episcopal Church in Black Mountain, North Carolina. Run by a former five-star-restaurant chef, the Welcome Table offers "a high-quality meal, using fresh and often local organic ingredients," under the slogan "Whoever will, may come." The poor and homeless are treated like "patrons of the finest restaurant . . . like dignified human beings deserving of the best food available." Bahnson remarks, "Why feed Jesus the dregs . . . when we could offer him fresh, organic vegetables?" The church collaborates with a local farmer, who runs a farm called The Lord's Acre, and who comments that all the shared work "makes social justice beautiful."[29] Imagine how we could make such a heavenly feast available in our parish communities, to the greater glory of God!

Happiness can also come from shared transportation. As a city dweller, I can remember times of unexpected shared joy and kindness that can happen on a bus or subway. One day in a Chicago subway station, a fantastic doo-wop quartet was singing harmonies to entertain the downtown crowds, their voices made even more beautiful echoing in the concrete tunnels. The happiness in the crowds of strangers was contagious. Another surefire way to use less fossil fuel is to access shared transportation. For several years, I've participated in carpools to work. Carpools are not always a barrel of fun. Someone ends up running late, or we'd like to leave work early but can't, or we simply notice the five to ten minutes "added" to the commute. However, the conversations and friendships of the carpool more than make up for it. How much richer it is to share a half-hour drive with real people as opposed to the radio!

These alternative patterns are not a matter of developing some fancy new technology. They are different ways of living we already know how to do. So, why not just do them? This brings us to a third issue: how we tend to prioritize the good of convenience over the good of protecting creation. As I said, carpools are not always the easiest things, nor are subways always places of uplifting encounter. They are *inconvenient* compared to commanding one's own vehicle. Food and fuel use that seem "necessary" may in fact be a matter of what we now call "convenience." The word derives from the Latin for "coming together"—we still "convene" meetings—but the word slowly evolved to indicate something that is easy. A little convenience is not a bad thing at all. However, our craving for ease and convenience over other values can easily go too far. If we are constantly opting for convenience, we are likely on the path to the deadly sin of sloth. We lose our ability to make the effort to develop meaningful skills ("convenience food") or to have exercise built into our lives ("convenient parking"). Always opting for convenience may also be a sign that the spiritual disease of speed is affecting our lives. Of course, we should not pretend that inconvenience is the path to ecological virtue—driving twenty miles each way to the diner serving sustainable food may not be smart, nor may be walking a mile in cold rain when you have a cold (hospital stays have a huge carbon footprint!).

Nevertheless, we should be alert to how our tendency toward convenience keeps us trapped in excess use.

Finally, a fourth step is to recognize and confront the structures that lead us to feel trapped into these cycles of overuse. To a considerable extent, there is no inherent reason why "fast" food has to be "unsustainable" food. There is no inherent reason why walking to places needs to be inconvenient—this is an example of a "structure of sin" that feels "built in" to many of our living environments. These structures are "rooted in personal sin"—hence, in the next chapter, we will turn to a second pattern, about our built environment, and explore the environmental issues related to this.

Our food and fuel are brought to us through what are called "market systems," or simply, "the market." Markets are humanly constructed things; they are good, but inevitably their construction means some things are incentivized and some things are disincentivized, usually based on the way we perceive the cost of different options. For example, "free roads" make driving seem cheaper than it is. Agricultural subsidies are given to farmers of large commodity crops, like corn and soybeans, but not to growers of fruits and vegetables (essentially a meat subsidy, since most of these crops are fed to livestock, if they are not turned into food additives like "high fructose corn syrup"). Attempts to develop housing projects that are more walkable and include small units and a mix of homes and businesses run into housing and zoning codes that regulate building. Building codes, help for farm stabilization, "socialist" roads—these are all reasonable choices that shape markets, but they are not always governed by attention to incentivizing environmental sustainability and may unwittingly disincentivize it.

More important, we need to recognize that as a whole market systems almost always leave some things out of the price—economists call these "externalities," and probably the most significant ones are the effects of environmentally unsustainable choices, especially ones that build up gradually over time through many, many small choices. Modern ideas about economics and private property came into being at a time when the urgent issue was to produce more basic goods, what seemed to be the perennial human problem. And they were wildly successful in doing so. However, at that time, nature's resources were seen to be basically infinite—the problem was "efficiently" converting those resources into necessary goods. Thus, the market is designed to maximize the allocative efficiency of production into what people want, without worrying much about whether nature can continue to provide these sources renewably or (perhaps more important) take care of the waste products, especially when they are dumped into what is usually called "the commons." Hence, many nations are now attempting systems that try to account for disposal in the cost of the goods—for example, forcing manufacturers to take back and recycle packaging and electronics (which of course incentivizes them to make less packaging and more durable products), or simply charging a tax on carbon emissions (which is what we commonly accept on products that potentially create social harm, like alcohol and tobacco and gambling).

One particular powerful way to confront these structures is to make the church a genuine alternative. The Christian life is not one of lonely purity and struggle. We are gathered by God as a people, and we can confront these problems both seriously and joyfully if we think about ways to act together. What can our local parish do to facilitate different and better choices in these areas? How can we act together to support local farmers and government officials trying to do the right thing?

Pope Benedict writes that abuse of nature by humanity "invites contemporary society to a serious review of its lifestyle, which, in many parts of the world, is prone to hedonism and consumerism, regardless of their harmful consequences" (*Caritas in Veritate* 51). Americans lead the world in categories like meat consumption and fossil fuel consumption; if the pope does not mean us, then who does he mean? It may be hard to connect his statement to a mid-sized car or a fast-food hamburger, but when we multiply these things daily and for hundreds of millions of users, we may begin to understand our "normal" lives more like an ancient bacchanal of constant unnecessary excess. Farmer Joel Salatin titled one of his books *Folks, This Ain't Normal*. Seeing this abnormality in our ordinary lives is not easy, for we are all accustomed to it, myself included. This is a case where our appetite for scale, speed, and the fulfillment of our own individual desires has created a pattern that seems normal to us—until we are confronted with nature's quite different patterns. Once we realize the proxies on which we rely for our daily bread and fuel, perhaps we too might see that even many parts of our daily lives are not normal—and seek change.

chapter 6

The Country and the City

The issue of environmental degradation challenges us to examine our life-style and the prevailing models of consumption and production, which are often unsustainable from a social, environmental, and even economic point of view. We can no longer do without a real change of outlook which will result in new life-styles.

—Benedict XVI[1]

The first pattern of our lives we explored was the search for calories. All life on earth requires calories. In the search for calories, species evolve forms of life together that inhabit physical environments in distinct ways. Creatures find and create dwelling places, or "habitats." In this chapter, we will look at the ecological questions raised by the human patterns of dwelling.

Do human beings have a "natural habitat"? We are going to approach this question by starting with two classic human habitats: the country and the city. As we saw in the earlier chapter on the Old Testament law, the Bible is mostly a book that arises out of and seems to endorse an agrarian way of life—settled life in what we call "the country." Despite our relative weakness

among creatures, we are invited by God to exercise skillful dominion in tending a garden. The laws given Israel are especially
directed to the rural life of small farmers. The "Promised Land"
is depicted in words emphasizing fertility and abundance, a land
flowing with milk and honey. Much of Jesus' ministry is exercised
among those who work that land or adjacent seas, and many of
his parables are about farming. Keep in mind that even the "large
cities" of his time were no more than fifteen thousand people!
Ancient Greek and Roman literature also contain the view that
humans dwell best as settled groups on the land, moving through
nature's cycles. Moreover, a strong strain of American national
consciousness is also attached to this vision, summed up by
Thomas Jefferson's famous ideal of the "yeoman farmer" as the
prime carrier of national virtues.

At the same time, the very word "civilization" comes from
the Latin *civitas,* for "city." Becoming "civilized" suggests that
human life achieves its true and highest potential in the urban
habitat, with its culture, communication, and community. What
does the Bible say about cities? It is true that parts of the Bible
can be read as a deeply antiurban text. Jacques Ellul famously
commented that in the Bible, the garden represents God's intention, but the city represents humanity's intention.[2] From Babel
to the Egyptian Pharaoh to the prophets like John the Baptist
crying out in the wilderness, the city can appear as a project of
human hubris and pride, where God is neglected and human beings exploited in a competitive race for glory. (In ancient times,
cities were rare and expensive and so usually existed as a kind
of built testimony to the glory and power of those who ruled.
In today's more democratic society, we might think of how cities promote vain competitions of display among individuals.)

Yet there is another strand too. As Tim Gorringe points out,
the Bible can also be read as a journey from garden to city.[3] Ellul
suggests that "it is in Jesus Christ that God adopts man's work"
of city building, and redirects it to God's ultimate intentions.[4]
After all, the hopes of the prophets always revolve around a
rebuilt *Jerusalem.* In the New Testament, Jesus' own life is a

journey from the rural hinterlands to the central city, and the Acts of the Apostles takes the early Christian movement from Jerusalem to the central city of all central cities, Rome. (Of course, these are also trips toward martyrdom!) Famously, the early Christian monks sought to flee the corruption of cities, only to have the desert turn into a city. And Revelation decisively images our final destiny and the conclusion of the universe in terms of a heavenly city.

Thus, in the Bible (as well as in Western thought more generally), we might sum up the testimony about human dwelling as a constant tension between two habitats, the country and the city, each seeming to present opportunities for flourishing and for destruction. This tension doesn't seem to disappear. In American literature, it is often depicted by contrasting the New Yorker Alexander Hamilton, who sought an America of commerce and finance, with Jefferson's "populist" defense of farming and pastoral nature as the American vision. Still today, many people who are not in any way farmers still aspire to a "country" lifestyle and are suspicious of cities; conversely, many people who have plenty of access to the wider culture through media still long to leave "dead-end towns" for the "bright lights" of the big city.

What does all this have to do with the environment? When we praise the beauty of nature and when we warn about unsustainable cycles of food and resource extraction, and complain about cars and frivolous consumer items, it can be tempting to think that in environmental terms, the right answer to this pattern question is to go "back to the land," out to the country. And yet there are some immediate paradoxes that come into view: urban areas of Europe and the United States often have far lower environmental footprints and far stronger support for environmental policies and practices! It is now often urban scientists who are far more attentive to the realities of environmental unsustainability than are people who yearn for "country life" and raise horses on hobby farms on the urban outskirts. Consider this example: A new Tractor Supply Company opened outside my town. Under its towering highway sign, it has a (plastic) horse roped to the pole—a supreme irony, since both the contents of the parking lot and the store itself are filled with endless machines that consume lots and lots of fossil fuel, but enhance the "rural lifestyle." Frankly, what is urgently needed today is an ability to see past these all-too-easy-to-stereotype contrasts so we can see how *both* patterns of life are intended to be in a healthy pattern of interdependence in order for humans and the creation to flourish.

When I speak here about country and city, I mean to talk about physical environments or habitats, that is, dwelling places. But these are also, crucially, forms of living together, dwelling in common in a particular place. They are forms of community, forms of "human ecology." Farm life is not solitary, by any means. Wendell Berry recalls the farm community of his youth, how during the arduous tobacco harvest "neighbors helped each other to bring together the many hands that lightened work. Thus, these times of hardest work were also the times of big meals and of much talk, storytelling, and laughter."[5] But city life is also a matter of being in a physical place with others. Much interesting commentary has recently been written on the fact that, despite our revolutionary technologies of connectivity, the development of culture, new ideas, and the like still flourishes in particular cities, which bring together a critical mass of diverse creativity.

Since these are forms of life together in a shared physical space, we necessarily make decisions about how to arrange and use the space. In pre-Elizabethan England, for example, many smallholders lived in villages and then went out to their assigned chunks of the fields, while using some of the grazing and forest land in common. Environmental writers have long debated the "enclosures" whereby shared pasture land was fenced off ("enclosed"). Did this enable people to take better care of stewarding that resource? Or did it encourage overuse because the land was now used for commodity farming, to sell at market, rather than as subsistence and neighborly exchange?

Decisions about how to arrange spaces continue to impact use. In our day, arrangement choices have large sustainability impacts. For example, recent surveys of various residential areas in and around Washington, DC, decisively demonstrate that use of public transportation is strongest with frequent train service, and that frequent train service can be economically viable and environmentally beneficial only in areas above a certain density of persons per square mile.[6] It is quite difficult to get shared transit to "work" once the density drops too far. Certainly when we think of the patterns of fossil fuel use as a key issue, dense development is much more sustainable. Yet it is also the case that density can put enormous stress on physical environments, especially in terms of producing waste. Moreover, overly dense environments threaten to leave no place for natural beauty. As with food and fuel, the point here is not to give absolute answers but to have us recognize how environmental issues are quite dependent on how we conceive of the ideal way we dwell together. Using fossil fuel or fertilizer can be fine, up to a point. Similarly, country and city should exist in a sustainable balance with one another.

In our society, our conceptions of land use are affected by two unique factors. Up until now, I have been speaking as if there are just two habitats: rural and urban. However, the modern world has created a third category, wilderness, and it tends to get a lot of attention from environmentalists, because it is understood to be "unspoiled nature." Before modern times, wilderness places were not idealized. True, in the Bible, the desert and the mountain often serve as important sites for communion with God, but it should be noted that these communions—from Sinai to the Transfiguration—are transient ones, and with good reason. Beautiful and awesome as they are, deserts, mountains, seas, and deep forests (think the Amazon) are extremely inhospitable places for human life. They may be wonderful for many other creatures (the Amazon rainforest is truly a marvel teeming with creatures), but they are evidently not our habitat (or if they are, then God must mean that there are way too many of us!). We are headed for environmental disorder when we overidealize these as "pure nature." Historian William Cronon notes that "wilderness embodies a dualistic vision in which the human is entirely outside the natural," thus, in admiring and preserving distant wilderness, "we give ourselves permission to evade responsibility for the lives we actually lead."[7] We then often neglect the beauty and care of the habitats in which humans actually live. Wendell Berry's friend from Kansas, Land Institute founder Wes Jackson, comments "with some anxiety on the people who charge blindly across Kansas and eastern Colorado, headed for the mountains west of Denver," worried that they "exclude unscenic places from nature and from the respect we accord to nature."[8] Worse, we can become tempted into the destructive hubris of building remote mountaintop enclaves or hurricane-exposed seaside houses, all in the name of "appreciating nature"!

A second unique problem comes from trying to "combine" what we perceive as "the best" of city and country life. This impulse has long dominated among the rich; the Roman elite of course lived in cities, but they also had their country villas to which they could "escape." They could enjoy the benefits of the city, but then retreat from its noise and lack of privacy to an abode of their own. But over the last one hundred years, particularly in America, the combination city/country ideal has been built in the rise of the habitat we usually call "suburban."[9] The suburbs have long been marketed as the truly pastoral form of urban life. Subdivisions have names like "Shady Meadows" or "Pleasant Acres" or "Oakwood Estates." One prominent terminus on the Washington Metro is called Shady Grove; another stop is Forest Glen. Needless to say, there are no shady groves or forest glens in these suburban stops!

It is hard to view suburban life as anything other than an unmitigated disaster from an environmental perspective, a "structure of sin" that creates environmental havoc despite the good intentions of individuals living in it.[10] The ecological destruction is disguised by the illusory trappings of rural nature, from large lawns to "quiet" cul-de-sac streets that go nowhere. Pastor Eric Jacobsen writes that Christians have tended to ignore issues of the built environment and "have not . . . taken seriously the physical form or context of existing cities as a viable model for our shared community life."[11] Jacobsen suggests our suburban model of development involves "worshiping false gods in the name of American values." These gods are false because, like all other false gods, "they consistently fail to deliver what they promise."[12] He names three in particular: individualism, independence, and freedom. The suburban dream of single-family homes on large lots, with a car in every garage, was supposed to free us from limitations imposed by denser urban development. Yet in many ways, suburbs fail to do this. They often suffer from a "cookie-cutter" uniformity and a commercial life dominated by large national chains; they make us depend on our cars (to the detriment in particular of children and the elderly, not to mention the environment); and they do not really allow us to "escape," especially as they themselves become more urbanized and developed. Worse, Jacobsen says, using "distance and avoidance" as the way of dealing with being "inconvenienced or annoyed by living, working, and playing in the company of our fellow human beings" seems utterly contrary to the Gospel admonition to love the neighbor, perhaps especially when he or she is a stranger or is in urgent need.[13] Gorringe notes how the problems of "natural ecology" also are manifest in the "human ecology" of the suburb, which "undeniably lacks both the community of the village and the energy of the town."[14]

Jacobsen notes that just as Christian churches began to recognize their responsibility for stewarding the natural environment, they should now develop a similar responsibility for built environments.[15] But in numerous ways, the two are in fact deeply intertwined. Key elements of Jacobsen's description of the value of cities are shared public spaces, walkability, and public art and parks. All of these are crucial elements of proper *scale*. Further, they contribute a considerable amount to reducing the need for large homes and constant driving, because they offer alternative public spaces close at hand. Catholic urban planner Philip Bess once said at a conference that he considered the half-mile walking radius to be a "natural law principle" that urban planners should follow in designing development.

Of course, there are other reasons people seek to escape to the suburbs. For example, concerns about crime and schools arise from a laudable desire to care for one's children (though they also may raise uncomfortable questions about our responsibility toward our neighbor's children). Even in suburban areas, however, newer development involves important planning choices that impact the environment. Most especially, the average size of new houses built in America has doubled in past decades, driving both spread-out lots and carbon-intensive energy bills.[16] Can we seek denser and more mixed-use development that would encourage smaller homes and walkability, not to mention sociability among neighbors? Can we locate this development in ways that offer easier transit access? Moreover, density also makes possible smaller models for the food business: small shops, markets, and restaurants with enough of a population close by to make a go of it. Finally, density in new development leaves more land to preserve farms closer to cities, making easier an interdependence between small growers and the urban population.

Patterns of dwelling have important implications in the country as well. All too often, rural life ends up as a kind of colony of the city. The city is dependent on the countryside for the resources it needs but consolidates power over the countryside to extract those resources as cheaply as possible. A more just and equitable relationship with a countryside actually *known* by city dwellers would also encourage better care for natural resources.

Pope John Paul II mentions "the need for urban planning" in order to achieve "an authentic human ecology" and replace "specific structures of sin" with "more authentic forms of living in community" (*Centesimus Annus* 38). Just as it is a mistake to believe that food and fuel "just show up" in our lives, so too our built environment and the geographies we inhabit are not "just there" but are chosen and developed in particular ways by human agents. In some ways, built environments are even more influential, since they usually represent a substantial long-term investment, making patterns difficult to change quickly. Thus, the pope counsels the need for "courage and patience" (ibid.). Nevertheless, patterns can and do change. Our care for creation requires that we make sure we move to change this pattern, allowing for sustainable use of the countryside by ensuring sustainable patterns for our cities.

chapter 7

Work and Play

On this earth there is room for everyone: here the entire human family must find the resources to live with dignity, through the help of nature itself . . . and through hard work and creativity. At the same time we must recognize our grave duty to hand on the earth to future generations in such a condition that they too can worthily inhabit it and continue to cultivate it. . . . . One of the greatest challenges facing the economy is to achieve the most efficient use—not abuse—of natural resources, based on a realization that the notion of "efficiency" is not value-free.

—Benedict XVI, *Caritas in Veritate* 50

Patterns of work and play, or work and what is classically known as "leisure," are our third item of practical inquiry. The way we work and play may seem very far from environmental issues, but in fact it is absolutely central. Wendell Berry writes that "work" is simply the name of our primary connection to the earth.[1] In Catholic social teaching, the importance of work and the dignity of labor have been central but much overlooked topics, especially in their relationship to the environment.[2] One could even argue that the patterns discussed in the past two chapters—about where we live and how we use food and fuel—

are themselves embedded in and dependent on the distinctive patterns of how we organize work and play. First, we will look at the peculiar characteristics of work as it has emerged in our society. Then we will look at a Catholic theology of work, in order to see how our present way of life is questioned, and how we can improve work in ways that demonstrate better care for the environment. Finally, we will look at how our work can lead to a distorted, overly consumptive view of leisure, also environmentally harmful.

Like where we live and where our food comes from, we can forget that ways of thinking about our daily labor are not fixed. Just one hundred years ago, the idea of a "weekend" was far from a given, sending children to work at young ages just seemed reasonable, and women were largely excluded from professions and confined to the home (unless they were very poor). All these things have changed dramatically . . . and they continue to evolve.

The most important and interesting development in our received pattern of work is the emergence of "*going to* work"—the idea that work involved leaving the household. Prior to modern times, work was usually tied up in one's social rank in the hierarchy, which directly related to one's familial ties; work was done in the context of that (extended) household—whether it be the lord's estate or one's own little freehold. Craftsmen owned their tools and established workshops where they lived, often taking apprentices into their households for many years. At the bottom of the hierarchy might be unskilled vagrants, who would work for occasional wage labor, or even slaves. The American system (most especially in the North) evolved from the English tradition of "small proprietors and shopkeepers," but with great opportunities in light of an abundance of land and the absence of aristocracy. This situation clearly established the small farmer and entrepreneur as the key figures of the American economy prior to the Civil War.

Yet this image can be more myth than reality; especially in the later nineteenth century, the advent of industrialized production, the railroads, corporate ownership, and the rise of manufactured consumer goods all combined to undermine household-based work. In its place, the nation shifted toward wage labor for the majority. While some sectors held off this sea change, to a greater or lesser extent, from the corner grocer to the family-owned and -run restaurant, the movement to wage labor was steady and seemingly inexorable. Why so? Clearly the primary reason was the efficiencies of scale made possible by large accumulations of expensive capital. No householder could make furniture like workers in a factory could, much less make cars or televisions or computers. We started "going to work."

We are likely to experience some sort of emotional reaction to this change—a sense of progress, or a wistful yearning for the family farm. But I invite us to focus on how this pattern shift in our work affected our relation to the environment. Certain issues have already been mentioned. "Going to work" meant working in large factories (scale) and racing with the clock (speed). It also meant transportation, unless one lived right next to the factory, which understandably was not attractive! But the key issue lies in the work itself, in both *what it does with the materials it uses* and *what it does to the people involved in the work*. Pope John Paul II, in his encyclical on work, made this distinction between what he called the "objective" and "subjective" dimensions of work (*Laborem Exercens* 5–6). Distortions of both dimensions can help us see more environmentally problematic patterns.

First, the objective dimension. Work ordinarily involves material goods, and too often modern work involves a careless use of these resources. Here, let us see how common the problem is. I admit I go through cheap, disposable pens without even noticing because they are so cheap; and I use them because I can basically ignore the problem of losing them, leaving them somewhere or misplacing them. I can be *careless* with them. Now it is true that industrial processes can be enormously efficient—that's part of the reason the pens are so cheap, and no doubt an equivalent number of handmade pens might use far *more* resources. But oftentimes there are many places in the process where "carelessness" is cheaper—wasting material goods is cheaper than the (more expensive) human labor that would go into being careful in conserving resources. Moreover, we are obviously simply producing *more* goods, even if each good is made more efficiently.

The ability to produce large amounts of goods very cheaply and efficiently naturally leads to the question of whether all these goods are needed. Economist Thorstein Veblen, at the turn of the century, praised what he called "the instinct of workmanship" embodied in industrial engineers who designed elegant machines making marvelous use of every aspect of materials. Such engineers abhorred waste, seeking "efficient use of the means at hand and adequate management of the resources available."[3] Veblen foresaw the possibility of an economy of abundance, where basic goods were made available to all through inexpensive, well-designed production. Unfortunately, Veblen wrote, enterprises were not run by these engineers but, rather, by "the salesmen"—who didn't actually want to make basic goods available to people as efficiently as possible and convinced people that they needed other, newer, better, "improved" goods with all sorts of bells and whistles. Indeed, making really *good* goods simply meant consumers kept what they had and didn't come back and buy more! So, the salesmen found ways to undermine the workmanship of the engineers. American automakers in the 1950s and 1960s famously began specifically designing their cars to wear out faster—"planned obsolescence"—and further helped this process along by introducing new "fashionable" design elements (which had no practical use) year after year.

Thus, one of the interesting but often overlooked questions of the last one hundred years is, given our enormous capacity to make goods quickly and easily and cheaply, why haven't we reached "abundance" or "enough"? A line of thinkers have responded similarly: because that would mean the end of economic profits, the extra money beyond labor compensation received by someone who provides something to you. We noted

Pope Francis's critique of the culture of waste. In his speech to mark World Environment Day, he said, "It is no longer [humankind] who commands, but money, money, cash commands. And God our Father gave us the task of protecting the earth—not for money, but for ourselves: for men and women. We have this task! Nevertheless men and women are sacrificed to the idols of profit and consumption: it is the 'culture of waste.'"[4] As he indicates here, the "culture of waste" is often driven by our economic system, which we will explore in our next chapter.

Many people respond (not wrongly) that if we listened to Francis, there would be no innovation, no new products. Capitalism requires what is usually called "creative destruction," that is, the replacement of some product or approach with something better. This is true, though the "destruction" part just assumes we can go on creating waste! This process inevitably involves considerable waste—take the obvious development of flat-screen TVs, which has led to the disposal of millions of working tube TVs. John Paul II complained of "the multiplication or continual replacement of the things already owned with others still better" and of the "throwing away" and "waste," when "an object already owned but now superseded by something better is discarded, with no thought of its possible lasting value in itself, nor of some other human being who is poorer" (*Sollicitudo Rei Socialis* 28). In the aggregate, these sorts of processes obviously involve considerable material pressure on resources. It would be difficult to imagine that they would not, since the ability to make money from the process has everything to do with the differential between raw material costs and the finished product. Some techno-optimists have suggested the online world heralds a new and "green" era: we will no longer really have to "go to work" because things will simply circulate around on the internet and be printed out on 3-D printers. But others have pointed out that the supposed "decoupling" of progress from the actual material consumption of more and more resources hasn't happened—indeed, quite the opposite. What is actually needed, the pope insists, is not more virtual reality games. Rather, we need the ability to distinguish between new needs that are actually worthwhile and ones that are frivolous.

This careless and profligate pattern of work also creates waste on the human side. Pursuing more and more cheap goods can often degrade work and the worker. Adam Smith noticed this about industrial work from the very beginning. He writes that, because of the division of labor, the life of the worker "comes to be confined to a very few simple operations," performed over and over, with "no occasion to assert his understanding." Because of this, he "generally becomes as stupid and ignorant as it is possible for a human creature to become."[5] Smith hoped that education might compensate. Others since him have hoped that we might simply be able to reduce how long we toil at mindless work, reaping the rewards of increased efficiency even as we submit to its mechanisms.

John Paul II insisted on the overriding importance of this "subjective dimension of work"—how work makes (or destroys) the worker. Work in our culture, he says, can often be measured purely in terms of material output, but the "fundamental and perennial heart of Christian teaching on human work" is "to serve to realize [the person's] humanity, to fulfill the calling to be a person that is his by reason of his very humanity" created in God's image. Thus, "the sources of the dignity of work are to be sought primarily in the subjective dimension, not in the objective one," for "in the first place work is 'for man' and not man 'for work'" (*Laborem Exercens* 6). Such dignity requires the priority of labor over capital, the rejection of "materialistic and economistic thought" in which work is treated as "merchandise," and a world where "each person is fully entitled to consider himself a part-owner of the great workbench" (ibid., 14). Work should be a key site for the development of the dignity of the person. But when work becomes monotonous and uninteresting, not only may we become careless about it, but we may also suffer as persons.

The tendency of modern work to be passive, degrading, and monotonous has had the effect of driving us into escape, into "leisure." In essence, modern wage work is a kind of trade-off: put in x number of hours of degrading servitude and receive a wage that we can do with as we please in our spare time. But often enough our leisure is just as degraded and commodified as our work. Worse, our leisure pursuits often involve cheap consumption that itself is environmentally and humanly destructive. We buy more and more electronic toys, mostly made in working conditions none of us would want to endure, and then when we replace them with newer toys, we ship the toxic e-waste back to poor countries where people eke out a meager living sorting through waste dumps for small amounts of recyclable materials. Or we "eat out"—an expensive thing to do, which is made cheaper and affordable only by the problematic agricultural practices described earlier. Leisure, which in theory could be environmentally benign, instead becomes wrapped up in more material commodities that are too often themselves produced in conditions of degraded work.

Because this whole cycle of unpleasant work for ongoing material consumption leaves us unsatisfied—as many studies show, consistent with John Paul II's idea that dignity comes from good work, not extra consumption—our final attempt to compensate is to speed up the cycle, amplify it, in the hopes that if it goes fast enough, we will be happy. If we are unhappy with our phone, we can get one that does even more. If we aren't satisfied with one hundred cable channel choices, we can order a package that gives us two hundred more. Ironically, both work and leisure then become subject to the problems of scale and speed that we discussed earlier, which are the main culprits in our loss of a sense of the beauty of the created world. Much is made of the fact that per capita energy use in America has remained largely flat since the early 1980s—but the fact is that our cars and new homes and refrigerators have gotten a lot more energy efficient since that time, and we have simply built bigger homes and found more and more devices to plug in. (This also neglects the extent to which we now import much more of our production, off-shoring not only the jobs but also the energy use.)

At a practical level, the cycle of dissatisfying, possibly even unnecessary, work and ever-faster commodified leisure is the driving force of many of the poor environmental choices we highlighted in the last two chapters. We become trapped in energy-intensive patterns of overwork and compensatory over-consumption. Economist Juliet Schor has written books about how both the "overworked" and the "overspent" American go together. While some have suggested that with the advent of an electronic economy, material goods become less important, Schor notes what she calls "the materiality paradox." While goods themselves are less important and more rapidly dis-posable, their symbolic value marking social status increases, and such "symbolic consumption relies heavily on fashion and novelty."[6]

The obvious solution to this cycle is to recognize that the ever-faster treadmill of monotonous work and commodified leisure is neither necessary for our social survival nor conducive to our social happiness—and so its environmental effects are that much more troubling. Numerous Christian authors have developed the idea of the Sabbath as a proper response to this cycle. But as we discussed earlier in chapter 3, Sabbath is not merely "more time away from work." It is the opportunity to live from sheer gratitude and delight. Norman Wirzba writes that "so much of our thinking about rest is off the mark because we lack the love that God has for everything." We are "bored" and "comfortably numb," and so we forget that the opposite of "rest" is not "work," but "restlessness." Ironically, we end up being "restless in both our work and our entertainment *because we find them unsatisfying* and not contributing to the fullness of life."[7]

What might such a Sabbath look like? There are many an-swers to this question, but all of them challenge our temptation to be constantly "on" and have constant "access" to whatever we want. Certainly, genuine rest after meaningful and diligent labor creating "good" would be spiritually valuable to us and would also give the planet a break. One wonders how our society's habits would look different if we still respected Sunday closing.

Indeed, in our internet age, imagine if Amazon was to make its site unavailable on Sundays! The prophet Amos chides those in ancient Israel whose desire for profit was so great that they eagerly awaited the end of the Sabbath:

> Hear this, you who trample upon the needy
>   and destroy the poor of the land:
> "When will the new moon be over," you ask,
>   "that we may sell our grain,
> And the sabbath,
>   that we may open the grain-bins?" (Amos 8:4-5)

But we no longer can wait even this long! Stores that used to open at 7 a.m. on the Friday after Thanksgiving now open on Thanksgiving itself. The selling must be constant.

Beyond practices of Sabbath, we must recognize that patterns of work and leisure are particularly wrapped up in larger social and political structures. Many of us may be able to exercise some choice over matters of what we eat and where we live; however, we may find ourselves unable to act individually in the workplace. We may desire to be more conscientious in our work or more careful about not wasting materials. Sadly, we may not have control to realize these changes.

More important, consider this: some people would be happy to make the trade-off of fewer work hours (and a lower salary) simply to enjoy more free time that really is "free" (i.e., not filled with purchased amusement). You may have read happily about meaningful work and peaceful leisure, but then thought, "Yeah, I wish I had that trade-off. But my job is my job—what can I do?" Few are given this choice as an option. European societies, with their lower environmental impacts, are far more worker-friendly, offering lengthier vacations, shorter hours, and considerably more maternity leave for the all-important task of raising children. These are all the result of regulations. Some economists point out that this makes those societies "less productive," and in simple material terms, that is true. But they have opted to shape modern work in a different way, and there is no reason why our society could not also consider such choices. Certainly, creation would benefit. But so would we.

chapter 8

The Global Economy

[T]he great challenge today is "to globalize" not only economic and commercial interests, but also the expectations of solidarity, with respect for and valuing the contribution of each component of society.

—Benedict XVI[1]

Every year, on the Day of the Dead, huge flocks of monarch butterflies fly into the forests of Central Mexico. Yet in 2012, the migration dropped to a record low of sixty million butterflies, and then in 2013, there were no butterflies at all. A few million straggled in later, but the flight of the butterflies seems to be nearing a total, abrupt collapse.[2] A similar phenomenon—called colony collapse disorder—has been affecting North American beekeepers over the last few years. Beekeepers would open their colonies to find no bees. Losses in the winter of 2012–13 totaled one-third of all colonies. One USDA official says, "The take home message is that we are very close to the edge"—for without bees and their unpaid labor of pollination, dozens of food crops cannot survive. Perhaps one-third of the food supply relies on this process, one that would be impossibly complicated to replicate by human artifice.[3] In both these cases, researchers cannot pinpoint a cause. Somehow the butterflies and the bees have not been able to sustain their natural patterns. Something is disrupting them as they go about their usual business.

I highlight these strange stories because the butterflies and the bees do not abide by our local designations of farm, town, even nation. Much of creation is transnational; the final pattern of human activity we need to examine is also one that goes far beyond national boundaries—and may seem just as mysterious: the global market economy. We will discuss two crucial aspects of how and why markets work, indicate why addressing these issues on the broadest possible scale is necessary for the environment, and finally relate the local and the global by explaining two key concepts of Catholic social thought that must go together: solidarity and subsidiarity.

Part of what is amazing about creation is its complexity. As we have seen earlier, we do not know exactly how everything works, and we probably would never be able to manage all of it. Erratic behavior by birds and bees suggests a mystery: something is going on, but what? Interestingly, the human structure that seems just as complex and mysterious is the thing we call "the market" or "the global economy." Like our patterns of eating, dwelling, and working, our economic structures are not given and fixed but have come about historically. In past ages, economies might have been commanded by kings and lords or worked out through elaborate traditional privileges and obligations. The term *oikonomia* is the Greek for "household" and referred to the tasks of the person in charge of managing the daily business of sustaining a household unit. Traditional systems of hereditary obligations, dictatorial command regimes, and even slaveholding still exist as economic practices—but today are often marginalized in favor of a vast system that no one, strictly speaking, runs. Instead, today's system is a matter of billions of free individual exchanges. We hear things like "consumer demand drives the economy." But this obscures the extent to which the system really does have oversight points and crucial junctures that shape it decisively. We might say that the economy clearly has "overseers" of a sort, but no true dictators. At these junctures, different choices can have quite hugely different environmental impacts. I highlight them in a little book like this because an understanding of them is particularly important for driving the democratic support, in church and world, for changes in these junctures of the global economy.

The first pattern to address within the global economy is the question of price. Why do things cost what they cost? In medieval times, prices were often set by rulers or guilds. Today, we sometimes act as if political leaders can manage prices. But we all vaguely know that what a free market means is that no one "sets" the price of anything—it is the market that sets the price. The market price system is one of the most remarkable discoveries in humanity's history, and one that we take for granted. That goods have prices seems as natural to us as the sun rising. But prices are not like flowers having petals or cats having tails. Where do these prices come from? And what do they do for us?

What is so powerful about the price system is this: fluctuating prices on an open market send signals to both producers and consumers to make decisions that optimally coordinate what producers produce and what consumers want. (This is the theory, anyway, and in a book this brief, I cannot go into the multiple scenarios of market manipulation and failure.) Prices are supposed to both reflect and affect supply and demand. A high price will reduce demand (so that people who have the strongest desire for something will be the most likely to get a scarce number), but it will also induce more supply (because there will be more production shifted into this high-demand good where a good price can be had). A "clearance" price will clear excess supply by increasing demand for a bargain: I might not have paid fifty dollars for that shirt, but I'll buy it for twenty dollars.

The reason the price system is so important for our discussion is that it works incredibly well to change behavior collectively not only of consumers but also of producers. And it does so *not* by mandating this or that exact behavior, but by *recalibrating the trade-offs* voluntarily made by hundreds of millions of market participants. So if we are concerned about the environment, scientist James Gustave Speth offers a simple rule: "It should be very expensive to do environmental harm and relatively inexpensive to do things that are environmentally harmless or restorative."[4] Don't tell people exactly what to do and not do—instead, shift the economic incentives to activities with the least environmental impact. Benedict XVI maintains, "The economic and social costs of using up shared environmental resources must be recognized with transparency and *borne by those who incur them*, and not by other peoples or future generations."[5]

This is why putting a global price on environmentally destructive actions is so important in the present context. In a sense, our current environmental situation could never have happened before because it was in fact quite expensive to do a lot of environmental harm (beyond a very localized level), and so very few people could do the harm. As we discussed in chapter 5, modern economics developed at a time when natural resources seemed abundant, almost limitless, and what was actually needed back in the seventeenth and eighteenth centuries was *incentives to use them*—for example, make land cheap, so people will make the effort themselves to "develop" the previously "worthless" land. The machines (capital) and workers (labor) were the real determiners of the price of goods. Today, we are still running basically that same software program in our economy, with the same results. We try to make it as cheap as possible to harvest raw materials and turn them into something people will buy. It is especially attractive to less developed nations to exploit these natural resources as fast as possible so they can exchange them for money from the developed world.

However, while we are running the same software, we are in a different situation, one in which protecting limited resources and dealing with an excessive waste stream need to be better accounted for in the price of goods. Economists call these "externalities"—some social benefit or harm that is a result of an economic process, but which is not included in the price. Societies should act to shift the price up or down, depending on whether the action creates more harm or good. Economies have for a long time dealt with externalities by either taxing them (if they are bad) or subsidizing them (if they are good). We hike tobacco taxes; we provide subsidies for home loans and children. Why? The former produces negative externalities; the latter produces positive ones (e.g., homeowners supposedly take better care of their own property and neighborhoods). We get less of what we tax and more of what we subsidize, and we do so by pushing on the price.

The outcome here is obvious: there should be more taxing and subsidizing for the protection of the environment. The price we pay should reflect our need to care for creation and use it sustainably. As Benedict XVI writes, "The international community and national governments are responsible for *sending the right signals* in order to combat effectively the misuse of the environment."[6] What is the best way to send such signals? Environmental writers debate three different ways to respond to problems: by regulation, by taxation, or by subsidies. Regulations often get considered first, largely because we are so sensitive to price, but regulations always run into the difficulty of how to direct very complex situations with many different people making many different choices. Regulation works well for straightforward environmental problems, such as stack scrubbers on smokestacks, eliminating poisonous pesticides like DDT, or banning chlorofluorocarbons globally (after the discovery of their role in creating a hole in the ozone layer). However, banning or even regulating things like fertilizers and fossil fuel use is very difficult. Subsidizing better alternatives can work, but it is sometimes hard to determine what the better alternatives are. It is not helpful to give large tax breaks for solar panels on roofs in cloudy areas! Hence, the better economic strategy is to tax the product with the negative outcome, and thus decrease demand for it, driving both consumers and producers to seek a variety of alternatives that work best in given situations. For example, taxing carbon makes sense because, as Dieter Helm writes, "When it comes to carbon, nobody particularly wants it. Demand for carbon is indirect—it is the goods and services within which carbon is embedded that count."[7] Both consumers and producers will then substitute less carbon-intensive goods. Helm's work suggests a carbon tax in part because it will push energy producers to move from the dirtiest fuel, coal, to other alternatives—cleaner fuels would have lower taxes, since the tax would be based on emissions. The same might be said for fertilizer: people actually want food, not fertilizer, and so by taxing nitrogen fertilizer, we not only encourage other methods of growing food but, more important, we encourage more careful, less wasteful use of fertilizers when needed, which would go a long way toward restoring a balance in the nitrogen cycle. In short, taxing externalities is often an excellent way to address environmental problems—like the ones we discussed—where the issue is not a straightforward evil, but rather an excess of something that might be used more sparingly.

Pricing environmental effects is one key to changing this pattern. The second aspect of the global economy that should receive attention is money, or the financial system. Money may be even more mysterious than prices. What exactly is it? In today's world, money is so-called "fiat" money—a world of floating exchange rates, where money is produced for the most part by banks lending it into existence. For much of human history, trade was facilitated by precious metals serving as money, culminating in the worldwide "gold standard" that ruled finance from the early nineteenth century through the 1930s, and to some extent after World War II, until Richard Nixon finally removed the dollar from gold in 1971. What matters about the gold standard was that the amount of money available was relatively fixed. Money was convertible by a government into gold, and therefore the amount of money available was controlled by the amount of gold. If a country sold more abroad than it bought, then it received gold; gold flowed out if it bought more than it sold. Gold essentially put a limit on the amount of currencies that could be in circulation. This was prudent, but also arbitrary; it created severe limitations for countries dealing with economic difficulties. Since the 1970s, money has essentially been priced by the worldwide financial markets, producing considerable bouts of instability along with considerable economic growth. Understanding the details of this system is problematic even for those initiated into it. Solutions to its problems can be oversimplified from one end—calls to "return to gold"—to the other—proposals that government debt problems can be solved simply by minting a trillion-dollar coin, since all our money is "fiat" money.

How do we understand the core issues and their relationship to environmental conservation? The core issues involve understanding wealth and debt within this system. Even "wealth" is a culturally varied phenomenon. Writer Michael Lewis tells the story of being introduced to an African tribal leader, who queried him about how many head of *cattle* he owned. This was a way of asking how wealthy he was, since in the African's culture owning cattle is both a source of income (selling their products) and capital (eating it or just selling the cows themselves). In medieval times, "wealth" might mean how much *land* a person owns, or even how many slaves or serfs they had. Today, we think of wealth in terms of how much a person "is worth," which usually involves owning a lot of *paper*. Some of this paper (which we call stock) is a claim to a share of the income and assets of some business, and some of it (bonds) is a claim to some portion of another person's future income, that is, we are a creditor to someone else, and that person is a debtor to us. We have excess funds we do not need to spend, and the debtor has promised to pay us back over time, with interest.

To lend at compounding interest is to believe that we have some money, and by giving it to someone else, we will get even more money back. This possibility of the limitless growth of paper is the key to our entire financial system. Herman Daly and John Cobb explain this in terms of the difference between accumulating a stock of pigs and accumulating credits against others:

> Compound interest or exponential growth of *negative* pigs [i.e., holding liens on others' pigs] presents no problem. But exponential growth of *positive* pigs soon leads to bedlam and ruin. Given the convenience of owning negative rather than positive pigs, the ruling passion of individuals in a modern economy is to convert [their] wealth into [others'] debt in order to derive a permanent future income from it . . . Individuals cannot amass all the physical supplies that they will require for maintenance during their old age, for like manna it would rot. Therefore they must convert their nonstorable surplus into a lien on future revenue by letting others consume and invest their surplus now in exchange for the right to share in the increased future revenue.[8]

Let us examine this point about debt closely. You will see it bears a striking resemblance to the points we made earlier about natural cycles of renewal: this process "works," but only up to a point. In this case, it works if the loan actually generates increased future revenue. Moreover, as Daly and Cobb point out, "because *some* people can live on interest it does not follow that *all* people could."[9] The mistake here is to take the old image of a landlord, who owns land and derives rent from it, and simply applying it to the ownership of money. The problem here is that money, unlike land, does not produce an annual harvest. But since money simply is numbers on a ledger, we can certainly *make believe* that it is producing that harvest.

Thus, in a financial system of paper claims to wealth, everything hangs on whether the debtors are using the resources of the creditors in ways that actually produce more "real wealth." That is, are the debtors like the landlord's tenants, producing a surplus, which both supports them and gives the landlord his or her share? When a prudent business takes a loan, it anticipates that it will use the loans to satisfy increased demand or improve its productivity, and if it does so, everyone wins. The creditor is a kind of temporary partner in the expanded income of the firm. However, if one takes a loan and can only pay back the interest, and must constantly "roll over" the loan, the ice becomes thin. The ice eventually breaks when the system becomes what we call a "Ponzi scheme"—the debtor cannot even pay back the interest but can only roll the interest over into an even bigger loan. That scheme either results in some kind of enslavement or (if that is not allowed) some kind of debt repudiation (what we call "bankruptcy," where some of the loan is simply written off).[10]

If, as was pointed out, a society is filled with more and more people attempting to live off their (paper) wealth as creditors, *the (paper) wealth, especially given compounding interest, is likely to outstrip the growth of "real wealth."* Such a situation has all the makings of a Ponzi scheme, in which (paper) growth must be maintained at all costs, lest the entire (paper) structure collapse. But how is this to be done? Unfortunately, it is here where the pigs (and cows and soil and forests) get the shaft. That is, the demands of compounding growth of (paper) wealth drive the maximal exploitation of the basis of all real wealth, the environment (including the body of the human person). This is not a difficult process to see. An indebted worker might sacrifice her health and her time in order to keep up with the bills. An indebted farmer may be driven to exploit his land for all its worth, because if he can't make the bank payment in September, he won't be around to see the land fifty years from now. An indebted country will be driven to exploit its natural resources in the same way. The finance system, originally conceived as a way to facilitate better use of real wealth (i.e., cows), now takes over the driver's seat. The real, finite economy ends up serving the paper, financial economy.

Thus, finance becomes the ultimate arbiter of scale—all natural and social processes must be run at a pace to keep up with the demands of compounding interest. Now in principle, the money economy cannot be allowed to grow at a faster rate than it is possible to sustainably grow the "real" economy, that is, growing crops and forests and the like at sustainable rates. Attempts to go faster must be burning "natural capital," like a company that borrows against and uses its assets, without accounting for maintenance and depreciation. Eventually, the company has a bunch of debts and a bunch of worn-out machines (and workers, most probably). The machines are worthless to sell, and they no longer can produce anything.

Why am I talking about all this in a theology book? It is quite important here to see how vividly the Bible condemns this system. It prohibits usury, that is, lending at interest, which in biblical times usually did not involve what we now call "investment." It insists on a land system where landholdings are widespread and cannot be accumulated by a small group of large landlords, which also incentivizes working the lands sustainably, since one can expect them to be in the family for a long time. And it rather severely condemns the whole idea of attempting to secure an easy future for oneself by "storing up" excess wealth. The "fool" is the one who, after reaping a rich harvest, says to himself, "This is what I shall do: I shall tear down my barns and build larger ones. There I shall store all my grain and other goods and I shall say to myself, 'Now as for you, you have so many good things stored up for many years, rest, eat, drink, be merry!'" (Luke 12:18-19). If we could sum up the Bible's "investment strategy," it is long-term, socially sustainable management of resources. Social and environmental sustainability for all takes precedence over the maximum accumulation for some.

It is very difficult to address large-scale environmental problems without tackling this problem of expanding finance as a driving force. The above examples of poor farmers and poor nations should make that all too clear. I do not think Chinese farmers use excess fertilizer and Chinese factories burn huge amounts of coal because they hate the environment or want to destroy it. They often do it in order to avoid or escape impoverishment. (The irony is that China is now a massive *creditor* nation, holding huge amounts of (paper) wealth, a great deal of it in the form of liens on the future incomes of the United States.) Unless we figure out better ways to help the impoverished—better ways than exploitative growth driven by debt finance—it is hard to escape the unsustainable destruction of the earth.

Recent popes have become increasingly critical of the present global financial system, led especially by Pope Paul VI. In his *Populorum Progressio,* he wrote that "the superfluous wealth of rich countries should be placed at the service of poor nations" (49) rather than drawing poor nations into supposed "free trade," which "taken by itself is no longer able to govern international relations" (58). Pope John Paul II criticized the "very typical," "all consuming desire for profit" and "the thirst for power" that is at the root of such "imperialism" (*Sollicitudo Rei Socialis* 37). Instead, the pope insists on "interdependence" and the "correlative" virtue of "solidarity," in which "we are all really responsible for all" (ibid., 38). He adds that "even the decision to invest in one place rather than another, in one productive sector rather than another is always a moral and cultural choice" (*Centesimus Annus* 36). In the wake of the 2007–2008 financial crisis, Pope Benedict XVI offered a massive critique of a global financial system "weighed down by malfunctions and dramatic problems" (*Caritas in Veritate* 21) and "marked by grave deviations and failures" by large businesses that "are almost exclusively answerable to their investors, thereby limiting their social value" (ibid., 40). Instead, he insists that globalization must be directed "so as to promote a person-based and community-oriented cultural process of worldwide integration that is open to transcendence" (ibid., 42). Ultimately, Benedict echoes the call of Pope John XXIII, indicating that "there is urgent need of a true world political authority" (ibid., 67). Pope Francis has connected all these criticisms in a striking way. In this system, he says, "the thirst for power and possessions knows no limits. In this system, which tends to devour everything which stands in the way of increased profits, whatever is fragile, like the environment, is defenseless before the interests of a deified market, which become the only rule." The "idolatry of money and the dictatorship of an impersonal economy," which we sadly "calmly accept," is "a new tyranny . . . invisible and often virtual, which unilaterally and relentlessly imposes its own laws and rules" (*Evangelii Gaudium* 55–56).

Perhaps a reader or two of this volume will be someone with actual legislative or financial power over the major institutions of the global economy. But for the rest of us, what does this mean? Here, we should consider Catholic social teaching's insistence on both solidarity and subsidiarity. These principles, especially in contemporary American politics, can seem at odds with one another. Solidarity is the idea that we must work together for the common good; subsidiarity is the idea that social and economic issues should not simply be addressed in a top-down fashion. As theologian Meghan Clark explains, "According to the principle of subsidiarity, decisions should be made *at the lowest level possible and the highest level necessary.* . . . Subsidiarity is an effort at balancing the many necessary levels of society—and at its best, the principle of subsidiarity navigates the allocation of resources by higher levels of society to support engagement and decision making by the lower levels. Despite how often it is stated—subsidiarity does NOT mean smaller is better."[11]

In our present situation, *solidarity* requires that we take responsibility for the economic system insofar as we participate in it. We must consider prices in light of the environment, for example, and do the same with our investments. Moreover, we must try to state this responsibility to elected political leaders, not just as individuals but as a church.

However, insofar as these economic issues invariably involve problems of scale—as in too big, too fast, too much growth, too many things—*subsidiarity* should insist that we turn our attention, energy, and resources to *local, reality-based alternatives* to this distorted, oversized way of organizing our material lives. Pope Benedict recommends "commercial enterprises based on mutualist principles and pursuing social ends," ones that include "quotas of gratuitousness and communion" (*Caritas in Veritate* 38–39). That is, the pope asks us to seek out businesses that are not simply about maximizing profit but instead aim at various "social" ends, supporting the common good actually within their business model. This approach is exemplified in hundreds of different kinds of projects: local food cooperatives, local land and investment trusts, banks and credit unions that actually stake themselves to the prosperity of the local economy, and so forth.

To sum up this chapter, it's difficult to be "green" environmentally without paying attention to what we do with our "green," meaning our money. Like our food system, our cities, and our work environment, this pattern might seem beyond our ability to understand and engage. But our faith leads us to be hopeful and to believe in the possibilities that can be made manifest if only we are willing to step up and make our meager contribution. I often think that one of the great parables for the Christian life is the story of the multiplication of the loaves and the fishes. We can easily become fixated on the miraculous power that Jesus displays, or the eucharistic echoes that are properly heard in the story. But what always strikes me is the boy who steps up; the disciples say, "There is a boy here who has five barley loaves and two fish; but what good are these for so many?" (John 6:9). What was the boy thinking? If someone says, "We need to feed all these people," and I have a little food, am I really going to stand up and say, "Well, here's my food"? Yet it seems clear from the story that the miraculous feeding is not "from nothing" but rather hinges on the boy stepping up. Let God do the multiplying. It's our role to step up with our loaves and fishes, even for a problem as large as the global economy.

Conclusion

Making Places Holy

The Eucharist itself powerfully illuminates human history and the whole cosmos. In this sacramental perspective, we learn day by day that every ecclesial event is a kind of sign by which God makes himself known and challenges us. The Eucharistic form of life can thus help foster a real change in the way we approach history and the world.

—Benedict XVI[1]

At the beginning of the third Eucharistic Prayer of the Mass, the priest says, "You are indeed holy, O Lord, / and all you have created / rightly gives you praise, / for through your Son our Lord Jesus Christ, / by the power and working of the Holy Spirit, / you give life to all things *and make them holy*" (italics added). The word "holy" can be one of those religious words that becomes so common and yet so churchy that we can use it almost automatically, without asking ourselves exactly what we mean when using it. What does it mean to say that God is at work making all things holy?

In this chapter, we conclude our journey by concentrating on holiness. Sometimes holiness can seem associated with only

117

certain things, or only certain people, but as the eucharistic prayer above indicates, all things can be made holy. And a major emphasis of Vatican II was reminding Catholics that all Christians—not just certain special groups—are called to a life of holiness. This book began by asking us to look around and take notice of nature. We conclude by recognizing our mission is not just to notice and admire, but to *consecrate* the world, make it holy, not by obliterating it, but by sanctifying it, making it new.

What is holiness? Return to the quote above. From just this prayer, we can see that holiness (a) comes from God, (b) is somehow beyond the sheer "existing" of things, and (c) applies to everything in creation. The particular "making holy" aimed at, as this prayer proceeds, is "making holy" the bread and wine. We say the bread and wine are "consecrated," which is essentially a synonym for "making holy." The term "to consecrate" comes from the Latin for sacred, to "con-sacred" something, to put the sacred with it, or to make something one with the sacred. Prior to being consecrated, the bread and wine exist and are perfectly good things. After, they are something more than this. What exactly?

Three further insights into what holiness means can be grasped by thinking through what Catholics are doing at Eucharist. First, the elements have been specially dedicated to God, and specifically to the praise and glory and honor of God. What we might call their natural purposes—say, nourishment, or even the ordinary fact that sharing food and drink in a group is an effective sign of friendship and conviviality—are not done away with, but they become directed toward a further, higher end: God and God's praise. Second, the elements become directed to this higher end through a special work of God: by being infused with the Holy Spirit, that is, the very Spirit that animates God's own life. The gifts actually share in the divine nature, "becoming" divine in the sense of participating in God's life and not just their own existence. Third, in becoming holy, the effect of a holy thing is to make it an instrument of *caritas*, the perfect love that is God's very nature. To say they become the Body and

Blood of Christ is to say they become alive as Christ is alive in the flesh, the perfect instrument of God's love for the world.

Consider these three aspects of holiness. They bring us to a deeper sense of what Catholics mean when professing belief in the "Real Presence"—because they are nothing other than the exact same things we believe about who Jesus is and how he lives! He is dedicated fully to God, shares in God's life through the work of the Holy Spirit, and is an instrument of the love of God for all. Hopefully, it is easy to take the next step here: what we say about the Eucharist is what we say about Jesus, and what we say about Jesus is what we say about *ourselves* as Catholics. We consume the Body of Christ and so "become holy" ourselves, becoming the Body of Christ that praises God, shares in the Holy Spirit, and lives as instruments of God's love.

We are all called to holiness. The Mass exists not to draw more people into the sanctuary, but to propagate the holiness, to radiate it outward, ultimately to all things. One of the greatest innovations of the Second Vatican Council was an emphasis on "the universal call to holiness." For many centuries, Catholicism had a kind of holiness "class hierarchy"—the term "holiness" seemed mostly to apply to the lives of ordained clergy and vowed members of religious communities. But in *Lumen Gentium*, its Dogmatic Constitution on the Church, the council spoke differently: "The Lord Jesus . . . preached holiness of life, which he both initiates and brings to perfection, to each and every one of his disciples no matter what their condition of life." He models this perfection of life and "sent the holy Spirit to all to move them interiorly to love God" and neighbor. In baptism, they "have been made sons and daughters of God . . . and partakers of the divine nature, and so are truly sanctified. They must therefore hold on to and perfect in their lives that holiness which they have received from God." Thus, the fathers conclude, "it is therefore quite clear that all Christians in whatever state or walk in life are called to the fullness of christian life and to the perfection of charity, and this holiness is conducive to a more human way of living even in society here on earth. . . .

The forms and tasks of life are many but there is one holiness" that is in all (40–41).[2]

What are the implications of this call to holiness? Here, we have to recognize a common misunderstanding of holiness, which is not wrong but is incomplete. Think of the common statement we hear, characterizing people as "holier than thou." It is clearly *not* a compliment! Whether or not this criticism is valid in any particular case, it points toward this incomplete way of understanding holiness. It is taking aim at a holiness that is focused on performing certain acts of ritual piety and perhaps even thinks of these ritual acts with a bit of spiritual pride and self-righteousness, as if these acts make one a "better" person in the eyes of God. Pope Francis, in one of his many memorable images, has suggested that the church needs to worry less about "making a mess" when it goes out into the world, also saying, "Let us ask ourselves: are we missionaries by our words, and especially by our Christian life, by our witness? Or are we Christians closed in our hearts and in our churches, sacristy Christians?"[3] Here, in expressing concern about "sacristy Christians," he is naming this same mistake, that "making ourselves holy" means carefully sealing ourselves up, like a museum piece that is kept immaculate by being completely isolated from any contact with the world, even with the air.

The problem is not the pious actions themselves, which are essential to holiness. Pope Francis spends hours of each day in prayer. Moreover, as we noted when discussing the sacramental worldview in an earlier chapter, a certain "separation" and distinction for sacred things makes sense. However, this can easily go too far, forgetting that the sacraments are ultimately instruments. For what? An escape from the world to some other one? By no means. The sacraments are instruments that bring about the three aspects of holiness explained here: dedication to God, sharing in the divine life, and living fully out of God's love.

In Vatican II's Dogmatic Constitution on the Church, each group within the church has a particular call, a different way of making this holiness manifest. For laypersons, this call is to the "making holy" of the world: "worshipping everywhere by their holy actions, the laity consecrate the world itself to God" (*Lumen Gentium* 34). The council fathers go on to explain this call: "The faithful must, then, acknowledge the inner nature and the value of the whole of creation and its orientation to the praise of God. They help one another, even through their secular activity, to achieve greater holiness of life, so that the world may be filled with the spirit of Christ and may the more effectively attain its destiny in justice, in love and in peace. The laity enjoy the principal role in the universal fulfillment of this task" (ibid., 36).

Our journey in this book has been dedicated to exactly this: to reveal "the inner nature and the value of the whole of creation and its orientation to the praise of God." That is, Catholics living in the world must not just *admire* the beauty of creation but must make it all holy, dedicate it all to the praise of God and the life of love. As we've said before, the point of Christian environmental care is not to worship nature or merely respect it but, rather, to *consecrate* it.

Let us then take as a first principle that when we consecrate something, both before and after the consecration, we do not destroy it. Quite the contrary. We treat it with deeper attention and reverence. To make places holy, we must relearn reverence for the created order as given by God. Just as God does not destroy our human nature in raising us to holiness but, rather, completes it, so too we must see the created order as something to be lifted up to holiness, not trampled down. Made radiant, not made barren. Our irreverence and carelessness are often due to our preoccupation with scale and speed and our own desires. It is also transferred to proxies, whereby we supposedly keep ourselves holy, while we rely on "dirty work" done by others. This renunciation of destruction and relearning of reverence is the basic conversion, the turning around, required for the practice of environmental holiness.

A second step is for us to begin to pay attention to the patterns of life discussed in the past four chapters. These are the key sites, the everyday "liturgies," in which we can practice this consecration (or the opposite!). This second step is more like an apprenticeship than a conversion. Ecological conversion means we simply must stop ignoring the destruction and unsustainability of our lives. But to recognize this and realize how abusive we are to God's order doesn't suddenly mean we start doing all the right things, especially for an issue as complex as this one. This should not be discouraging. Jesus presents a very vivid, sharp, demanding path of holiness and, at the same time, insists on the need to practice it with constant mercy, compassion, and struggle in the right direction. Thus, we are likely to have to live for a while with a thorn in our side, a set of patterns that is problematic but that we continue to work on improving. We can learn over time, with help, how to make the pursuit of "our daily bread" an occasion for holiness rather than desecration. We can look at where we live and our communities to move them in directions that better harmonize with the ecosystems of city and country. We should begin to transform our workplaces and our leisure in directions that honor and reverence the material goods that facilitate them. And we can bank, invest, and vote in ways that recognize the highest end is not economic accumulation, but making the world a place where material creation serves the praise of God.

To make something holy is to direct it to its ultimate purpose. The sequence of the previous chapters is not accidental. Our present society orients all these patterns toward the final one, economic growth, as the ultimate common end of material activity. We have all too easily come to equate progress in "the goods life" as the good life. Brad Gregory writes, "Amid the hyperpluralism of divergent truth claims, metaphysical beliefs, moral values, and life priorities, ubiquitous practices of consumerism are more than anything else the cultural glue that holds Western societies together." We may disagree and debate many things as a society, but "most people in the early twenty-first century will want more and better stuff, whatever their beliefs about the Life Questions."[4]

This secular version of "progress" is really the root problem for the environment. It involves a kind of false god, an idol in which we all too fervently believe and trust. As such, it becomes a *replacement* for our real destiny. This progress is a false version of true Christian hope. In his encyclical *Spe Salvi*, Pope Benedict writes, "It is not that faith is simply denied; rather it is displaced onto another level—that of purely private and other-worldly affairs—and at the same time it becomes somehow irrelevant for the world" (17). Once faith becomes otherworldly, then worldly "faith in progress" becomes identified with scientific reason and the freedom to use the results of that reason in any way we wish. For Francis Bacon, the original thinker of the modern scientific approach, "It is clear that the recent spate of discoveries and inventions is just the beginning; through the interplay of science and praxis, totally new discoveries will follow, a totally new world will emerge, the kingdom of man. He even put forward a vision of foreseeable inventions—including the aeroplane and the submarine" (ibid.). Yet, are these inventions what mark true human progress? The pope rightly suggests that the use of human reason and freedom "becomes human only if it is capable of directing the will along the right path, and it is capable of this only if it looks beyond itself. Otherwise, man's situation, in view of the imbalance between his material capacity and the lack of judgment in his heart, becomes a threat for him *and for creation*" (ibid., 23; italics added). Our understanding of what constitutes genuine material progress—and the appropriate and reasonable limits on it—must be measured by a higher standard, that of holiness and love. Material progress itself cannot serve as the standard.

The pope makes our responsibilities for changing these patterns clear: "There is a need . . . to move beyond a purely consumerist mentality in order to promote forms of agricultural and industrial production capable of respecting creation and satisfying the primary needs of all."[5] We are called to turn this order around; the economy should serve good, durable, careful work; work should serve our places and communities; and our places should serve to provide us with the basic material substance that we need to sustain our lives. This is why the environmental movement has so often focused on the importance of food. Of course, this focus on food can become distorted by the same partial approach to holiness that can infect Catholic religious rituals. People can become "holier-than-thou" about food choices and can develop a kind of fastidiousness that does not really get at the root of the problem. Yet the importance of eating should not be underestimated. It is profoundly significant that the central religious act in Catholicism is that of eating and drinking. As Norman Wirzba reminds us, "We eat to live, knowing that without food we will starve and die. But to eat we must also kill, realizing that without the death of others—microbes, insects, plants, animals—we have no food."[6] We inevitably practice "sacrificial eating" and, in so doing, participate in what theologians call "the paschal mystery," the mystery of how life emerges one's death, how giving up one's life produces abundant life. Therefore, it is a mistake to think that the Eucharist must be either sacrifice or meal. It is a sacrificial meal; and the same pattern can then inspire our other eating, our dwelling, our working, and even our economic exchange.

In his book *The Gift of Good Land*, Wendell Berry's title essay is an eloquent summing up of the possibilities for making places holy. He recalls the Promised Land as "a gift because the people who are to possess it did not create it."[7] Above all, we must come to see everything—including all of nature—is not "ours" but is received from God. He then notes that, in giving the land, God instructs his people in the importance of "neighborliness" and "good husbandry"[8]—that is, sharing and good quality, careful work. We must be instructed and trained in care of neighbor and in skill. But finally, Berry writes, "That is not to suggest we can live harmlessly, or strictly at our own expense; we depend upon other creatures and survive by their deaths. To live, we must daily break the body and shed the blood of Creation. When we do this knowingly, lovingly, skillfully, reverently, it is a sacrament. When we do it ignorantly, greedily, clumsily, destructively, it is a desecration. In such desecration we condemn ourselves to spiritual and moral loneliness, and others to want."[9]

We depend on God's good creation for our life. We see its beauty and goodness, lament our own inability to receive it well, and hope that God might renew us and refashion this bond of dependence in ways that glorify God and rejoice with the neighbor. That renewal is what we mean by making all things holy; when we do it together (as we must), we are being the church, the people called to be a sacrament of Christ for the world. In caring for creation, and in refashioning our patterns of life, this call to holiness should enliven us collectively to joyfully give ourselves so that others—and all creation—might live.

Notes

Introduction (pages ix–xviii)

1. Benedict XVI, Letter to Bartholomew I, Ecumenical Patriarch on the Occasion of the Sixth Symposium on "Religion, Science, and the Environment" Focusing on the Amazon River, July 6, 2006, in *The Environment*, ed. Jacquelyn Lindsey (Huntington, IN: Our Sunday Visitor, 2012), 20–21.

2. Wendell Berry, *Sex, Economy, Freedom, and Community* (New York: Pantheon/Random House, 1993), 19, 23.

3. Francis Bacon, "The Great Instauration," in *The Philosophy of the 16th and 17th Centuries*, ed. Richard H. Popkin (New York: Free Press, 1966), 100.

4. Wendell Berry, *The Way of Ignorance* (Berkeley, CA: Counterpoint, 2005), 55.

5. Francis, Audience to Representatives of the Communications Media, March 16, 2013, http://www.vatican.va/holy_father/francesco/speeches /2013/march/documents/papa-francesco_20130316_rappresentanti -media_en.html.

6. Pope Francis, Mass for the Beginning of the Petrine Ministry of the Bishop of Rome, March 19, 2013, http://www.vatican.va/holy_father /francesco/homilies/2013/documents/papa-francesco_20130319 _omelia-inizio-pontificato_en.html.

Chapter 1—Beauty (pages 3–11)

1. Benedict XVI, *Verbum Domini* (apostolic exhortation), par. 108, in *The Environment*, ed. Jacquelyn Lindsey (Huntington, IN: Our Sunday Visitor, 2012), 146.

2. Mircea Eliade, *The Sacred and the Profane: The Nature of Religion* (New York: Harper and Row, 1961), 20.

3. Hans Urs von Balthasar, *The Glory of the Lord, Volume 1: Seeing the Form*, trans. Erasmo Leiva-Merikakis (San Francisco: Ignatius Press, 1982).

4. William P. Brown, *The Seven Pillars of Creation: The Bible, Science, and the Ecology of Wonder* (New York: Oxford University Press, 2010), 4.

5. Anthony Ciorra, *Beauty: A Path to God* (New York: Paulist Press, 2013), 17.

6. John O'Donohue, *Beauty* (New York: HarperCollins, 2004), 14.

7. Ibid.

8. On "the grammar of creation," see David Cloutier, "Working with the Grammar of Creation: Benedict XVI, Wendell Berry, and the Unity of the Catholic Moral Vision," *Communio* 37 (2010): 606–33.

9. Jame Schaefer, *Theological Foundations for Environmental Ethics: Reconstructing Patristic and Medieval Concepts* (Washington, DC: Georgetown University Press, 2009), 69.

10. Bill McKibben, *Oil and Honey: The Education of an Unlikely Activist* (New York: Henry Holt, 2013), 73.

11. Ibid., 77.

12. Balthasar, *Seeing the Form*, 37, 118; cited in Edward Oakes, SJ, *Pattern of Redemption: The Theology of Hans Urs von Balthasar* (New York: Continuum, 1994), 144, 148.

13. Balthasar, *Theo-Logic, Volume 1: Truth of the World*, trans. Adrian J. Walker (San Francisco: Ignatius Press, 2000), 107; quoted in Matthew T. Eggemeier, "A Sacramental Vision: Environmental Degradation and the Aesthetics of Creation," *Modern Theology* 29, no. 3 (July 2013): 353.

14. Schaefer, *Theological Foundations*, 45.

15. C. S. Lewis, *The Four Loves* (New York: Harcourt Brace, 1960).

16. Schaefer, *Theological Foundations*, 44.

17. Ibid., 75.

18. Chet Raymo, *The Path: A One-Mile Walk Through the Universe* (New York: Walker, 2003), 2.

19. Ibid., 5–6.

20. Michael Pollan, *The Omnivore's Dilemma* (New York: Penguin, 2006), 126.

21. Ibid., 188.

22. Ibid., 208, 213.

23. See Ellen F. Davis, *Scripture, Culture, and Agriculture: An Agrarian Reading of the Bible* (New York: Cambridge University Press, 2009), 104, on the overall productivity of small farms.

Chapter 2—Losing Our Place (pages 12–26)

1. Benedict XVI, Common Declaration with Ecumenical Patriarch Bartholomew I, Apostolic Journey to Turkey, November 30, 2006, in *The Environment*, ed. Jacquelyn Lindsey (Huntington, IN: Our Sunday Visitor, 2012), 26.

2. Anthony Ciorra, *Beauty: A Path to God* (New York: Paulist Press, 2013), 6.

3. Jared Diamond, *Collapse: How Societies Choose to Succeed or Fail* (New York: Penguin, 2005).

4. E. F. Schumacher, *Small Is Beautiful: A Study of Economics as if People Mattered* (London: Abacus, 1973), 29.

5. John O'Donohue, *Beauty* (New York: HarperCollins, 2004), 25.

6. Norman Wirzba, *Food and Faith: A Theology of Eating* (New York: Cambridge University Press, 2011), 27.

7. David Harvey, *The Condition of Postmodernity* (Malden, MA: Blackwell, 1990), 240.

8. Kelly Johnson, "God Does Not Hurry," in *God Does Not . . . Entertain, Play "Matchmaker," Hurry, Demand Blood, Cure Every Illness*, ed. D. Brent Laytham, 68–72 (Grand Rapids, MI: Brazos Press, 2009).

9. Wirzba, *Food and Faith*, 27.

10. Michael Northcott, *The Environment and Christian Ethics* (Cambridge: Cambridge University Press, 1996), 205. For an analysis of this "great disembedding," see Charles Taylor, *Modern Social Imaginaries* (Durham, NC: Duke University Press, 2004), 49–67.

11. Jame Schaefer, *Theological Foundations for Environmental Ethics: Reconstructing Patristic and Medieval Concepts* (Washington, DC: Georgetown University Press, 2009), 88.

12. See the maps at the National Atmospheric Deposition Program, "Annual NTN Maps by Year," http://nadp.sws.uiuc.edu/ntn/annualmapsbyyear.aspx.

13. K. Lee Lerner and Brenda Wilmoth Lerner, eds., "Cumberland Mountain Area Scarred by Strip Mining," in *Environmental Issues: Essential Primary Sources* (Farmington Hills, MI: Thomson Gale, 2006), 391–92.

14. US EPA, "EPA Makes Announcement on Two Proposed West Virginia Mountaintop Coal Mines," January 5, 2010, http://yosemite.epa.gov/opa/admpress.nsf/0/84636183A97CED24852576A20069961A.

15. Lerner and Lerner, "Cumberland Mountain," 392.

16. US EPA, "Mid-Atlantic Mountaintop Mining," http://www.epa.gov/Region3/mtntop/.

17. US EPA, "EPA Makes Announcement"; "Spruce No. 1 Mine," http://www.epa.gov/region03/mtntop/spruce1.html.

18. Dan Barry, "As the Mountaintops Fall, a Coal Town Vanishes," *New York Times* (April 12, 2011).

19. John W. Miller and Rebecca Smith, "Gas Boom Aside, Coal Isn't Dead," *Wall Street Journal* 263, no. 5 (January 7, 2014): B1, B4.

20. Michael Northcott, *A Political Theology of Climate Change* (Grand Rapids, MI: Eerdmans, 2013), 54.

Chapter 3—Basic Theology I: Creation and Covenant
(pages 27–40)

1. Benedict XVI, General Audience, August 26, 2009, in *The Environment*, ed. Jacquelyn Lindsey (Huntington, IN: Our Sunday Visitor, 2012), 115.

2. USCCB, "Renewing the Earth," in *And God Saw That It Was Good: Catholic Theology and the Environment*, ed. Drew Christiansen and Walter Grazer, 228 (Washington, DC: USCCB, 1991).

3. Michael Northcott, *The Environment and Christian Ethics* (Cambridge: Cambridge University Press, 1996), 164.

4. Northcott, *The Environment*, 174.

5. Ellen F. Davis, *Scripture, Culture, and Agriculture: An Agrarian Reading of the Bible* (New York: Cambridge University Press, 2009), 58.

6. E. F. Schumacher, *Small Is Beautiful: A Study of Economics as if People Mattered* (London: Abacus, 1973), 10–11.

7. Davis, *Scripture, Culture*, 59–60.

8. Northcott, *The Environment*, 180.

9. Davis, *Scripture, Culture*, 60.

10. Norman Wirzba, *Food and Faith: A Theology of Eating* (New York: Cambridge University Press, 2011), 43.

11. Ibid., 45.

12. Ibid., 47.

13. Karl Barth, *Church Dogmatics* III/4, ed. G. W. Bromiley and T. F. Torrance (Edinburgh: T&T Clark, 1961), 54.

14. Benedict, "If You Want to Cultivate Peace, Protect Creation," 2010 World Day of Peace Message, 6, http://www.vatican.va/holy_father /benedict_xvi/messages/peace/documents/hf_ben-xvi_mes_20091208 _xliii-world-day-peace_en.html.

15. Davis, *Scripture, Culture*, 82.

16. Northcott, *The Environment*, 184.

17. Davis, *Scripture, Culture*, 109, citing Lev 25:4-5.

18. Northcott, *The Environment*, 192.

19. Walter Brueggemann, "Land: Fertility and Justice," in *Theology of the Land*, ed. Bernard Evans and Gregory Cusack, 59 (Collegeville, MN: Liturgical Press, 1987).

20. Davis, *Scripture, Culture*, 70.

21. Ibid., 75.

22. Robert Karl Gnuse, *You Shall Not Steal: Community and Property in the Biblical Tradition* (Maryknoll, NY: Orbis, 1985), 7.

Chapter 4—Basic Theology II: Redemption and Renewal
(pages 41–52)

1. Benedict XVI, *Sacramentum Caritatis* (apostolic exhortation), 92, http://www.vatican.va/holy_father/benedict_xvi/apost_exhortations /documents/hf_ben-xvi_exh_20070222_sacramentum-caritatis_en.html.

2. Lynn White Jr., "The Historical Roots of Our Ecologic Crisis," *Science* 155 (March 10, 1967): 1203–7.

3. *Catechism of the Catholic Church*, 2nd ed. (Libreria Editrice Vaticana, 1997), 1046–47.

4. Michael Northcott, *The Environment and Christian Ethics* (Cambridge: Cambridge University Press, 1996), 209.

5. Irenaeus, *Against Heresies* II, 9, 1, in *The Scandal of the Incarnation: Irenaeus Against the Heresies*, ed. Hans Urs von Balthasar, 33 (San Francisco: Ignatius Press, 1990).

6. Ibid., 53.

7. USCCB, "Renewing the Earth," in *And God Saw That It Was Good: Catholic Theology and the Environment*, ed. Drew Christiansen and Walter Grazer, 231 (Washington, DC: USCCB, 1991).

8. M. Therese Lysaught, "Love and Liturgy," in *Gathered for the Journey: Moral Theology in Catholic Perspective* (Grand Rapids, MI: Eerdmans, 2007), 24–42.

9. Joseph A. Fitzmyer, *The Gospel According to Luke*, The Anchor Bible, vol. 28A (Garden City, NY: Doubleday, 1985), 1204.

10. Craig Blomberg, *Neither Poverty Nor Riches: A Biblical Theology of Possessions* (Downers Grove, IL: InterVarsity Press, 2000), 83.

11. Sondra Ely Wheeler, *Wealth as Peril and Obligation: The New Testament on Possessions* (Grand Rapids, MI: Eerdmans, 1995), 123–27.

12. Luke Timothy Johnson, *Sharing Possessions: What Faith Demands*, 2nd ed. (Grand Rapids, MI: Eerdmans, 2011), 23.

13. Helen Rhee, *Loving the Poor, Saving the Rich* (Grand Rapids, MI: Baker Academic, 2012), xx.

14. Glen Stassen and David Gushee, *Kingdom Ethics: Following Jesus in Contemporary Context* (Downers Grove, IL: InterVarsity Press, 2003), 411, 417.

15. Thomas Aquinas, *Summa Theologiae* I–II, q. 2, a. 1.

16. On the poor as a sacrament in the biblical text, see Gary Anderson, *Charity: The Place of the Poor in the Biblical Tradition* (New Haven, CT: Yale University Press, 2013).

Transition—What, Then, Shall We Do? (pages 53–59)

1. Mike Berners-Lee, *How Bad Are Bananas? The Carbon Footprint of Everything* (Vancouver, BC: Greystone Books, 2011).

2. Lori Bongiorno, *Green, Greener, Greenest: A Practical Guide to Making Eco-Smart Choices a Part of Your Life* (New York: Penguin, 2008).

3. James Garvey, *The Ethics of Climate Change* (New York: Continuum, 2008), 141.

4. Benedict XVI, "If You Want to Cultivate Peace, Protect Creation," 2010 World Day of Peace Message, 10, http://www.vatican.va/holy_father/benedict_xvi/messages/peace/documents/hf_ben-xvi_mes_20091208_xliii-world-day-peace_en.html.

5. An excellent example can be found in Steven Bouma-Prediger's chapter "What's Wrong with the World?" in *For the Beauty of the Earth: A Christian Vision for Creation Care*, 2nd ed. (Grand Rapids, MI: Baker Academic, 2010), 23–55.

6. Ibid., 29–32.

7. Christiana Peppard, *Just Water: Theology, Ethics, and the Global Water Crisis* (Maryknoll, NY: Orbis, 2014), 21–22.

8. Ibid., 22.

Chapter 5—Food and Fuel (pages 63–84)

1. Benedict XVI, Message to the Director General of the Food and Agriculture Organization for the Celebration of World Food Day, October 16, 2006, in *The Environment*, ed. Jacquelyn Lindsey (Huntington, IN: Our Sunday Visitor, 2012), 24.

2. William Wan, "Desperate for clean air, Chinese get creative," *Washington Post* (January 26, 2014).

3. "One Nation, Under Smog," *Time* 182, no. 19 (November 4, 2013): 11. For more data, see Simon Denyer, "Advocates Hail Action by China on Air Pollution," *Washington Post* (February 3, 2014).

4. Alan L. Olmstead and Paul W. Rhode, "The Transformation of Northern Agriculture, 1910–1990," in *The Cambridge Economic History of the United States: Volume III: The Twentieth Century*, ed. Stanley L. Engerman and Robert E. Gallman, 693 (Cambridge: Cambridge University Press, 2000).

5. US EPA, "Ag 101: Demographics," http://www.epa.gov/oecaagct /ag101/demographics.html.

6. US Department of Labor Bureau of Labor Statistics, "American Time Use Survey—2012 Results," http://www.bls.gov/news.release /atus.nr0.htm. Note that some Americans do not watch TV, but for ones that do, the average consumed every day is 3.54 hours.

7. Centers for Disease Control and Prevention, "Overweight and Obesity: Adult Obesity Facts," http://www.cdc.gov/obesity/data/adult .html.

8. Bill McKibben, *Deep Economy* (New York: Henry Holt, 2007), 42.

9. Jason McKenney, "Artificial Fertility: The Environmental Costs of Industrial Fertilizers," in *The Fatal Harvest Reader*, ed. Andrew Kimbrell, 123 (Washington, DC: Island Press, 2002).

10. Scott Bontz, "Nn," *Land Report*, no. 107 (Fall 2013): 14.

11. McKenney, "Artificial Fertility," 125.

12. Ibid., 125–26.

13. Ibid., 125–27; Bontz, "Nn," 22–23.

14. J. Rockstrom et al., "A Safe Operating Space for Humanity," *Nature* 461 (September 24, 2009): 473.

15. *World Almanac 2013*, ed. Sarah Janssen (New York: Infobase Learning, 2013), 324, from US Department of Energy data.

16. Aradhna K. Tripati et al., "Coupling of CO2 and Ice Sheet Stability over Major Climate Transitions of the Last 20 Million Years," *Science* 326 (December 4, 2009): 1394–97, cited in Michael Northcott, *A Political Theology of Climate Change* (Grand Rapids, MI: Eerdmans, 2013), 23.

17. This data is widely available. A recent, balanced summary is provided in William Nordhaus, *The Climate Casino: Risk, Uncertainty, and Economics for a Warming World* (New Haven, CT: Yale University Press, 2013).

18. Ibid.

19. Rob Dietz and Dan O'Neill, *Enough Is Enough: Building a Sustainable Economy in a World of Finite Resources* (San Francisco: Berrett-Koehler, 2013), 23.

20. Bryan Walsh, "The Future of Oil," *Time* 179, no. 14 (April 9, 2012): 28–35.

21. Wendell Berry, "Faustian Economics," in *What Matters: Economics for a Renewed Commonwealth* (Berkeley, CA: Counterpoint, 2010), 41.

22. Wendell Berry, "Conservation Is Good Work," in *Sex, Economy, Freedom, and Community* (New York: Pantheon/Random House, 1993), 37.

23. Ibid., 39.

24. Ibid., 36.

25. Benedict XVI, General Audience, August 26, 2009, in *The Environment*, 114, italics added.

26. Pope Francis, General Audience, Saint Peter's Square, June 5, 2013, http://www.vatican.va/holy_father/francesco/audiences/2013/documents/papa-francesco_20130605_udienza-generale_en.html.

27. United States Conference of Catholic Bishops, "Reflections on the Energy Crisis: A Statement by the Committee on Social Development and World Peace," April 2, 1981, http://www.usccb.org/issues-and-action/human-life-and-dignity/environment/upload/moral-principles-from-1981-energy-statement.pdf.

28. Tim Kasser, *The High Price of Materialism* (Cambridge, MA: MIT Press, 2002).

29. Fred Bahnson and Norman Wirzba, *Making Peace with the Land: God's Call to Reconcile with Creation* (Downers Grove, IL: IVP Books, 2012), 103.

Chapter 6—The Country and the City (pages 85–93)

1. Benedict XVI, "If You Want to Cultivate Peace, Protect Creation," 2010 World Day of Peace Message, 11, http://www.vatican.va/holy_father/benedict_xvi/messages/peace/documents/hf_ben-xvi_mes_20091208_xliii-world-day-peace_en.html.

2. Jacques Ellul, *The Meaning of the City* (Grand Rapids, MI: Eerdmans, 1970).

3. Timothy J. Gorringe, *A Theology of the Built Environment: Justice, Empowerment, Redemption* (Cambridge: Cambridge University Press, 2002), 119.

4. Ellul, *Meaning of the City*, 176–77.

5. Wendell Berry, *Sex, Economy, Freedom, and Community* (New York: Pantheon/Random House, 1993), 55.

6. Robert E. Griffiths, *2011 TPB Geographically-Focused Household Travel Surveys Initial Results*, 2011 National Capital Region Transportation Planning Board Meeting (Washington, DC: Metropolitan Washington Council of Governments, 2012) .

7. William Cronon, "The Trouble with Wilderness; or Getting Back to the Wrong Nature," in *Uncommon Ground: Rethinking the Human Place in Nature*, ed. William Cronon, 80–81 (New York: W. W. Norton, 1996).

8. Berry, *Sex, Economy*, 28.

9. In 1900, only 15.4 percent of the population lived in towns ringing a central city; by 1990, that number was 46.2 percent and growing rapidly. See Carol E. Heim, "Structural Changes: Regional and Urban," in *The Cambridge Economic History of the United States: Volume III: The Twentieth Century*, ed. Stanley L. Engerman and Robert E. Gallman (Cambridge: Cambridge University Press, 2000), 144.

10. David Cloutier, "American Lifestyles and Structures of Sin," in *Environmental Justice and Climate Change*, ed. Jame Schaefer and Tobias Winright (Lanham, MD: Rowman & Littlefield, 2013), 218–26.

11. Eric O. Jacobsen, *Sidewalks in the Kingdom: New Urbanism and the Christian Faith* (Grand Rapids, MI: Brazos Press, 2003), 14.

12. Ibid., 21.

13. Ibid., 28.

14. Gorringe, *Built Environment*, 133.

15. Jacobsen, *Sidewalks*, 68.

16. Julie Polter, "Attack of the Monster Houses," *Sojourners* 36, no. 3 (2007): 38–42.

Chapter 7—Work and Play (pages 94–103)

1. Wendell Berry, *Sex, Economy, Freedom, and Community* (New York: Pantheon/Random House, 1993), 35.

2. The most important example is Pope John Paul II's neglected encyclical *Laborem Exercens*.

3. Thorstein Veblen, *The Instinct of Workmanship* (New York: Macmillan, 1914), 31.

4. Pope Francis, General Audience, Saint Peter's Square, June 5, 2013, http://www.vatican.va/holy_father/francesco/audiences/2013 /documents/papa-francesco_20130605_udienza-generale_en.html.

5. Adam Smith, *The Wealth of Nations* (New York: Modern Library, 1937), 734.

6. Juliet Schor, *Plenitude: The New Economics of True Wealth* (New York: Penguin, 2010), 27.

7. Fred Bahnson and Norman Wirzba, *Making Peace with the Land: God's Call to Reconcile with Creation* (Downers Grove, IL: IVP Books, 2012), 38–39, italics added.

Chapter 8—The Global Economy (pages 104–16)

1. Benedict XVI, Address to Members of the "Centesimus Annus-Pro Pontifice" Foundation, May 31, 2008, in *The Environment*, ed. Jacquelyn Lindsey (Huntington, IN: Our Sunday Visitor, 2012), 72.

2. Jim Robbins, "The Year the Monarch Didn't Appear," *New York Times* 163, issue 56330 (November 24, 2013): Sunday Review, 9.

3. Bryan Walsh, "The Plight of the Honeybee," *Time* 182, no. 8 (August 19, 2013): 26–31.

4. James Gustave Speth, *The Bridge at the End of the World* (New Haven, CT: Yale University Press, 2008), 100.

5. Benedict XVI, General Audience, August 26, 2009, in *The Environment*, 115; italics added.

6. Benedict XVI, "If You Want to Cultivate Peace, Protect Creation," 2010 World Day of Peace Message, 7; italics added, http://www.vatican.va/holy_father/benedict_xvi/messages/peace/documents/hf_ben-xvi_mes_20091208_xliii-world-day-peace_en.html.

7. Dieter Helm, *The Carbon Crunch* (New Haven, CT: Yale University Press, 2012), 179.

8. Herman Daly and John Cobb, *For the Common Good*, 2nd ed. (Boston: Beacon Press, 1994), 423–24; italics added.

9. Ibid., 424; italics added.

10. John Cassidy, *How Markets Fail* (New York: Farrar, Straus, and Giroux, 2009), 207–12.

11. Meghan Clark, "Subsidiarity Is a Two-Sided Coin," CatholicMoral Theology.com, March 8, 2012, http://catholicmoraltheology.com/subsidiarity-is-a-two-sided-coin/.

Conclusion—Making Places Holy (pages 117–25)

1. Benedict XVI, *Sacramentum Caritatis* (apostolic exhortation), 92, http://www.vatican.va/holy_father/benedict_xvi/apost_exhortations/documents/hf_ben-xvi_exh_20070222_sacramentum-caritatis_en.html.

2. Quotations from Vatican II documents are taken from Austin Flannery, ed., *Vatican Council II: Constitutions, Decrees, Declarations; The Basic Sixteen Documents* (Collegeville, MN: Liturgical Press, 2014).

3. Francis, General Audience, Saint Peter's Square, October 16, 2013, http://www.vatican.va/holy_father/francesco/audiences/2013/documents/papa-francesco_20131016_udienza-generale_en.html.

4. Brad S. Gregory, *The Unintended Reformation: How a Religious Revolution Secularized Society* (Cambridge: Harvard University Press, 2012), 236.

5. Benedict XVI, "If You Want to Cultivate Peace, Protect Creation," 2010 World Day of Peace Message, 10, http://www.vatican.va/holy_father/benedict_xvi/messages/peace/documents/hf_ben-xvi_mes_20091208_xliii-world-day-peace_en.html.

6. Norman Wirzba, *Food and Faith: A Theology of Eating* (New York: Cambridge University Press, 2011), 110–11.

7. Wendell Berry, *The Gift of Good Land* (Berkeley, CA: Counterpoint, 1981), 270. I am grateful to Norman Wirzba's aforementioned book for calling attention to this passage from Berry.

8. Ibid., 272.

9. Ibid., 281.

Bibliography

Anderson, Gary. *Charity: The Place of the Poor in the Biblical Tradition*. New Haven, CT: Yale University Press, 2013.

Bacon, Francis. "The Great Instauration." In *The Philosophy of the 16th and 17th Centuries*, edited by Richard H. Popkin, 83–109. New York: Free Press, 1966.

Bahnson, Fred, and Norman Wirzba. *Making Peace with the Land: God's Call to Reconcile with Creation*. Downers Grove, IL: IVP Books, 2012.

Balthasar, Hans Urs von. *The Glory of the Lord. Volume 1: Seeing the Form*. Translated by Erasmo Leiva-Merikakis. San Francisco: Ignatius Press, 1982.

Barth, Karl. *Church Dogmatics* III, 4. Edited by G. W. Bromiley and T. F. Torrance. Edinburgh: T&T Clark, 1961.

Benedict XVI. *The Environment*. Edited by Jacquelyn Lindsey. Huntington, IN: Our Sunday Visitor, 2012.

———. "If You Want to Cultivate Peace, Protect Creation." 2010 World Day of Peace Message. http://www.vatican.va/holy_father /benedict_xvi/messages/peace/documents/hf_ben-xvi_mes _20091208_xliii-world-day-peace_en.html.

Berners-Lee, Mike. *How Bad Are Bananas? The Carbon Footprint of Everything*. Vancouver, BC: Greystone Books, 2011.

Berry, Wendell. "Faustian Economics." In *What Matters: Economics for a Renewed Commonwealth*, 41–54. Berkeley, CA: Counterpoint, 2010.

———. *The Gift of Good Land*. Berkeley, CA: Counterpoint, 1981.

———. *Sex, Economy, Freedom, and Community*. New York: Pantheon/ Random House, 1993.

———. *The Way of Ignorance*. Berkeley, CA: Counterpoint, 2005.

Blomberg, Craig. *Neither Poverty Nor Riches: A Biblical Theology of Possessions*. Downers Grove, IL: InterVarsity Press, 2000.

Bongiorno, Lori. *Green, Greener, Greenest: A Practical Guide to Making Eco-Smart Choices a Part of Your Life.* New York: Penguin, 2008.

Bontz, Scott. "N^n." *Land Report*, no. 107 (Fall 2013): 10–24.

Bouma-Prediger, Steven. *For the Beauty of the Earth: A Christian Vision for Creation Care.* 2nd ed. Grand Rapids, MI: Baker Academic, 2010.

Brown, William P. *The Seven Pillars of Creation: The Bible, Science, and the Ecology of Wonder.* New York: Oxford University Press, 2010.

Brueggemann, Walter. "Land: Fertility and Justice." In *Theology of the Land*, edited by Bernard Evans and Gregory Cusack, 41–68. Collegeville, MN: Liturgical Press, 1987.

Cassidy, John. *How Markets Fail.* New York: Farrar, Straus, and Giroux, 2009.

Centers for Disease Control and Prevention. "Overweight and Obesity: Adult Obesity Facts." http://www.cdc.gov/obesity/data/adult .html.

Ciorra, Anthony. *Beauty: A Path to God.* New York: Paulist Press, 2013.

Clark, Meghan. "Subsidiarity Is a Two-Sided Coin." CatholicMoral Theology.com. March 8, 2012. http://catholicmoraltheology .com/subsidiarity-is-a-two-sided-coin/.

Cloutier, David. "American Lifestyles and Structures of Sin: The Practical Implications of Pope Benedict XVI's Ecological Vision for the American Church." In *Environmental Justice and Climate Change*, edited by Jame Schaefer and Tobias Winright, 215–35. Lanham, MD: Rowman & Littlefield, 2013.

———. "The Problem of Luxury in the Christian Life." *Journal of the Society of Christian Ethics* 32 (2012): 3–20.

———. "Working with the Grammar of Creation: Benedict XVI, Wendell Berry, and the Unity of the Catholic Moral Vision." *Communio* 37 (2010): 606–33.

Cronon, William. "The Trouble with Wilderness; or Getting Back to the Wrong Nature." In *Uncommon Ground: Rethinking the Human Place in Nature*, edited by William Cronon, 69–90. New York: W. W. Norton, 1996.

Daly, Herman, and John Cobb. *For the Common Good.* 2nd ed. Boston: Beacon Press, 1994.

Davis, Ellen F. *Scripture, Culture, and Agriculture: An Agrarian Reading of the Bible.* New York: Cambridge University Press, 2009.

Denyer, Simon. "Advocates Hail Action by China on Air Pollution." *Washington Post* (February 3, 2014).

Diamond, Jared. *Collapse: How Societies Choose to Succeed or Fail*. New York: Penguin, 2005.

Dietz, Rob, and Dan O'Neill. *Enough Is Enough: Building a Sustainable Economy in a World of Finite Resources*. San Francisco: Berrett-Koehler, 2013.

Eggemeier, Matthew T. "A Sacramental Vision: Environmental Degradation and the Aesthetics of Creation." *Modern Theology* 29, no. 3 (July 2013): 338–60.

Eliade, Mircea. *The Sacred and the Profane: The Nature of Religion*. New York: Harper and Row, 1961.

Ellul, Jacques. *The Meaning of the City*. Grand Rapids, MI: Eerdmans, 1970.

Fitzmyer, Joseph A. *The Gospel According to Luke*. The Anchor Bible. Vol. 28A. Garden City, NY: Doubleday, 1985.

Francis. Audience to Representatives of the Communications Media. March 16, 2013. http://www.vatican.va/holy_father/francesco /speeches/2013/march/documents/papa-francesco_20130316 _rappresentanti-media_en.html.

———. General Audience. Saint Peter's Square. June 5, 2013. http://www .vatican.va/holy_father/francesco/audiences/2013/documents /papa-francesco_20130605_udienza-generale_en.html.

———. General Audience. Saint Peter's Square. October 16, 2013. http://www.vatican.va/holy_father/francesco/audiences /2013/documents/papa-francesco_20131016_udienza-generale _en.html.

———. Mass for the Beginning of the Petrine Ministry of the Bishop of Rome. March 19, 2013. http://www.vatican.va/holy_father /francesco/homilies/2013/documents/papa-francesco_20130319 _omelia-inizio-pontificato_en.html.

Garvey, James. *The Ethics of Climate Change*. New York: Continuum, 2008.

Gnuse, Robert Karl. *You Shall Not Steal: Community and Property in the Biblical Tradition*. Maryknoll, NY: Orbis, 1985.

Gorringe, Tim J. *A Theology of the Built Environment: Justice, Empowerment, Redemption*. Cambridge: Cambridge University Press, 2002.

Gregory, Brad S. *The Unintended Reformation: How a Religious Revolution Secularized Society*. Cambridge: Harvard University Press, 2012.

Griffiths, Robert E. *2011 TPB Geographically-Focused Household Travel Surveys Initial Results*. 2011 National Capital Region Transportation Planning Board Meeting. Washington, DC: Metropolitan Washington Council of Governments, 2012.

Harvey, David. *The Condition of Postmodernity*. Malden, MA: Blackwell, 1990.

Heim, Carol E. "Structural Changes: Regional and Urban." In *The Cambridge Economic History of the United States: Volume III: The Twentieth Century*, edited by Stanley L. Engerman and Robert E. Gallman, 93–190. Cambridge: Cambridge University Press, 2000.

Helm, Dieter. *The Carbon Crunch*. New Haven, CT: Yale University Press, 2012.

Irenaeus. *Against Heresies*. In *The Scandal of the Incarnation: Irenaeus Against the Heresies*, edited by Hans Urs von Balthasar. San Francisco: Ignatius Press, 1990.

Jacobsen, Eric O. *Sidewalks in the Kingdom: New Urbanism and the Christian Faith*. Grand Rapids, MI: Brazos Press, 2003.

Johnson, Kelly. "God Does Not Hurry." In *God Does Not . . . Entertain, Play "Matchmaker," Hurry, Demand Blood, Cure Every Illness*, edited by D. Brent Laytham, 63–81. Grand Rapids, MI: Brazos Press, 2009.

Johnson, Luke Timothy. *Sharing Possessions: What Faith Demands*. 2nd ed. Grand Rapids, MI: Eerdmans, 2011.

Kasser, Tim. *The High Price of Materialism*. Cambridge, MA: MIT Press, 2002.

Lerner, K. Lee, and Brenda Wilmoth Lerner, eds. "Cumberland Mountain Area Scarred by Strip Mining." In *Environmental Issues: Essential Primary Sources*, 391–92. Farmington Hills, MI: Thomson Gale, 2006.

Lewis, C. S. *The Four Loves*. New York: Harcourt Brace, 1960.

Lysaught, M. Therese, "Love and Liturgy." In *Gathered for the Journey: Moral Theology in Catholic Perspective*, edited by M. Therese Lysaught and David M. McCarthy, 24–42. Grand Rapids, MI: Eerdmans, 2007.

McKenney, Jason. "Artificial Fertility: The Environmental Costs of Industrial Fertilizers." In *The Fatal Harvest Reader*, edited by Andrew Kimbrell, 121–29. Washington, DC: Island Press, 2002.

McKibben, Bill. *Deep Economy*. New York: Henry Holt, 2007.

———. *Oil and Honey: The Education of an Unlikely Activist*. New York: Henry Holt, 2013.

Miller, John W., and Rebecca Smith. "Gas Boom Aside, Coal Isn't Dead." *Wall Street Journal* 263, no. 5 (January 7, 2014): B1–B4.

National Atmospheric Deposition Program. "Annual NTN Maps by Year." http://nadp.sws.uiuc.edu/ntn/annualmapsbyyear.aspx.

Nordhaus, William. *The Climate Casino: Risk, Uncertainty, and Economics for a Warming World*. New Haven, CT: Yale University Press, 2013.

Northcott, Michael. *The Environment and Christian Ethics*. Cambridge: Cambridge University Press, 1996.

———. *A Moral Climate: The Ethics of Global Warming*. Maryknoll, NY: Orbis, 2007.

———. *A Political Theology of Climate Change*. Grand Rapids, MI: Eerdmans, 2013.

Oakes, Edward, S.J. *Pattern of Redemption: The Theology of Hans Urs von Balthasar*. New York: Continuum, 1994.

O'Donohue, John. *Beauty*. New York: HarperCollins, 2004.

Olmstead, Alan L., and Paul W. Rhode, "The Transformation of Northern Agriculture, 1910–1990." In *The Cambridge Economic History of the United States: Volume III: The Twentieth Century*, edited by Stanley L. Engerman and Robert E. Gallman, 693–742. Cambridge: Cambridge University Press, 2000.

"One Nation, Under Smog." *Time* 182, no. 19 (November 4, 2013): 11.

Peppard, Christiana. *Just Water: Theology, Ethics, and the Global Water Crisis*. Maryknoll, NY: Orbis, 2014.

Pollan, Michael. *The Omnivore's Dilemma*. New York: Penguin, 2006.

Polter, Julie. "Attack of the Monster Houses." *Sojourners* 36, no. 3 (2007): 38–42.

Raymo, Chet. *The Path: A One-Mile Walk Through the Universe*. New York: Walker, 2003.

Rhee, Helen. *Loving the Poor, Saving the Rich*. Grand Rapids, MI: Baker Academic, 2012.

Robbins, Jim. "The Year the Monarch Didn't Appear." *New York Times* 163, issue 56330 (November 24, 2013): Sunday Review, 9.

Rockstrom, J. et al. "A Safe Operating Space for Humanity." *Nature* 461 (September 24, 2009): 472–75.

Rubio, Julie Hanlon. "Moral Cooperation with Evil and Social Ethics." *Journal of the Society of Christian Ethics* 31 (2011): 103–22.

Schaefer, Jame. *Theological Foundations for Environmental Ethics: Reconstructing Patristic and Medieval Concepts*. Washington, DC: Georgetown University Press, 2009.

Schor, Juliet. *Plenitude: The New Economics of True Wealth*. New York: Penguin, 2010.

Schumacher, E. F. *Small Is Beautiful: A Study of Economics as if People Mattered*. London: Abacus, 1973.

Smith, Adam. *The Wealth of Nations*. New York: Modern Library, 1937.

Speth, James Gustave. *The Bridge at the End of the World*. New Haven, CT: Yale University Press, 2008.

Stassen, Glen, and David Gushee. *Kingdom Ethics: Following Jesus in Contemporary Context*. Downers Grove, IL: InterVarsity Press, 2003.

Stuart, Tristram. *Waste: Uncovering the Global Food Scandal*. New York: W.W. Norton, 2009.

Taylor, Charles. *Modern Social Imaginaries*. Durham, NC: Duke University Press, 2004.

Tripati, Aradhna K. et al. "Coupling of CO2 and Ice Sheet Stability over Major Climate Transitions of the Last 20 Million Years." *Science* 326 (December 4, 2009): 1394–97.

Union of Concerned Scientists. *Cooler Smarter: Practical Steps for Low-Carbon Living*. Washington, DC: Island Press, 2012.

USCCB. "Renewing the Earth." In *And God Saw That It Was Good: Catholic Theology and the Environment*, edited by Drew Christiansen and Walter Grazer, 223–43. Washington, DC: USCCB, 1991.

US Department of Labor Bureau of Labor Statistics. "American Time Use Survey—2012 Results." http://www.bls.gov/news.release/atus.nr0.htm.

US EPA. "Ag 101: Demographics." http://www.epa.gov/oecaagct/ag101/demographics.html.

———. "EPA Makes Announcement on Two Proposed West Virginia Mountaintop Coal Mines." January 5, 2010. http://yosemite.epa.gov/opa/admpress.nsf/0/84636183A97CED24852576A20069961A.

———. "Mid-Atlantic Mountaintop Mining." http://www.epa.gov/Region3/mtntop/.

Veblen, Thorstein. *The Instinct of Workmanship*. New York: Macmillan, 1914.

Walsh, Bryan. "The Future of Oil." *Time* 179, no. 14 (April 9, 2012): 28–35.

———. "The Plight of the Honeybee." *Time* 182, no. 8 (August 19, 2013): 26–31.

Wan, William. "Desperate for clean air, Chinese get creative." *Washington Post* (January 26, 2014).

Wheeler, Sondra Ely. *Wealth as Peril and Obligation: The New Testament on Possessions*. Grand Rapids, MI: Eerdmans, 1995.

White, Lynn, Jr. "The Historical Roots of Our Ecologic Crisis." *Science* 155 (March 10, 1967): 1203–7.

Wirzba, Norman. *Food and Faith: A Theology of Eating.* New York: Cambridge University Press, 2011.

World Almanac 2013. Edited by Sarah Janssen. New York: Infobase Learning, 2013.